THE UNITED STATES

The Thirteen Original Colonies

Connecticut
Delaware
Georgia
Maryland
Massachusetts
New Hampshire
New Jersey
New York
North Carolina
Pennsylvania
Rhode Island
South Carolina
Virginia

DON'T KNOW MUCH ABOUT®

THE
★ 50 ★
STATES

KENNETH C. DAVIS
ILLUSTRATED BY RENÉE ANDRIANI

HarperCollins*Publishers*

Acknowledgments

An author's name goes on the cover of a book. But behind that book are a great many people who make it all happen. I would like to thank all of the wonderful people at HarperCollins who helped make this book a reality, including Susan Katz, Kate Morgan Jackson, Barbara Lalicki, Harriett Barton, Rosemary Brosnan, Meredith Charpentier, Anne Dunn, Dana Hayward, Fumi Kosaka, Marisa Miller, Rachel Orr, and Katherine Rogers. I would also like to thank David Black, Joy Tutela, and Alix Reid for their friendship, assistance, and great ideas. My wife, Joann, and my children, Jenny and Colin, are always a source of inspiration, joy, and support. Without them, I could not do my work.

I especially thank April Prince for her devoted efforts and unique contributions. This book would not have been possible without her tireless work, imagination, and creativity.

This is a Don't Know Much About® book. Don't Know Much About®
is the trademark of Kenneth C. Davis.

The excerpt on page 46 is from A GIRL FROM YAMHILL:
A MEMOIR ©1988 by Beverly Cleary.
Used with the permission of HarperCollins Publishers.

Don't Know Much About® the 50 States
Copyright © 2001 by Kenneth C. Davis
Printed in the U.S.A. All rights reserved.
www.harperchildrens.com

Library of Congress Cataloging-in-Publication Data
Davis, Kenneth C.
    Don't know much about the 50 states / by Kenneth C. Davis ; illustrated by Renée Andriani.
        p.   cm. — (Don't know much)
    Summary: Provides assorted facts about each of the fifty states in question and answer format.
    ISBN 0-06-028607-5 — ISBN 0-06-028608-3 (lib. bdg.)
    1. U.S. states—Miscellanea—Juvenile literature.   2. United States—Miscellanea—Juvenile literature.
[1. United States—Miscellanea.   2. Questions and answers.]   I. Williams-Andriani, Renée, ill.
II. Title.   III. Series.
E180 .D38   2000   00-022442
973—dc21

Design by Charles Yuen
3   4   5   6   7   8   9   10
❖
First Edition

Answers to quiz on back cover: 1) California, 2) Rhode Island, 3) Alaska, 4) Virginia, 5) Delaware, 6) Hawaii, 7) New York, 8) Utah, 9) Oklahoma, 10) Florida

INTRODUCTION

Look at the American flag. Some people call it Old Glory. Others call it the Stars and Stripes. What do you see?

Fifty white stars. That's easy: one for each state. But there are only thirteen stripes. Why? Those red and white stripes stand for the thirteen states that made up the United States of America in 1776, the year that America was born. And you thought thirteen was an unlucky number!

Those stripes tell us that the United States of America was not always such a big place. Our country began more than two hundred years ago, when the thirteen places we now call states were still called colonies ruled by the King of England.

The thirteen separate states agreed to stand together as one nation to help one another. That is how our country got its name—the United States of America. The U.S.A. has changed a great deal during the past two centuries. Over the years more states were added. That is called being "admitted to the Union," just like getting an admission ticket to the movies. Only the states didn't have to buy a ticket.

Don't Know Much About® the 50 States tells the story of each of those states. But this book is not just filled with dates of admission and names of capitals. Like every *Don't Know Much About®* book, it is loaded with questions and answers about unusual people and places that make learning about the states a lot of fun.

ALABAMA

NICKNAME:	THE YELLOWHAMMER STATE
STATEHOOD:	1819
CAPITAL:	MONTGOMERY
STATE FLOWER:	CAMELLIA
STATE BIRD:	YELLOWHAMMER

What do Alabama's nickname and state bird have to do with the Civil War?

Alabama is called the Yellowhammer State because during the Civil War, many of the state's soldiers wore bright yellow uniforms. (Not very good camouflage, huh?) The yellowhammer was chosen as the state bird because it is the same color as those uniforms.

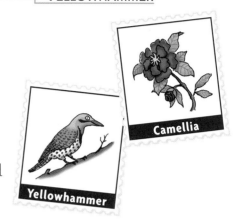

Yellowhammer

Camellia

Where should you go if you want to feel out of this world?

To Space Camp in Huntsville! There you can learn about space missions and feel what it's like to tumble around weightless in space. The space rocket that first sent people to the moon was invented at the Alabama Space and Rocket Center at Huntsville.

Where did Rosa Parks purposely park herself, in protest?

Alabama gets its name from a Choctaw Indian word that means "vegetation gatherers."

In 1955 Rosa Parks was arrested for sitting in an empty seat on a bus in Montgomery. The seat was for white people only, and Parks is black. Her courage started a yearlong boycott during which black people refused to ride buses. Eventually they won the right to sit wherever they wanted.

ALASKA

AK

NICKNAME: THE LAST FRONTIER
STATEHOOD: 1959
CAPITAL: JUNEAU
STATE FLOWER: FORGET-ME-NOT
STATE BIRD: WILLOW PTARMIGAN

Willow ptarmigan

Forget-me-not

What could you do with 425 Rhode Islands?

Fit them inside Alaska! Alaska is America's largest state. If you put it on top of the lower forty-eight states, it would stretch all the way from California to Florida. Not only is it the largest state, but it also has the highest mountain (Mount McKinley), the northernmost point in the United States (Point Barrow), and the most coastline of any state. It's no wonder "Alaska" comes from an Aleutian (Eskimo) word, *alakshak*, meaning "great land"!

Alaska is closer to Russia (two miles away at one point) than it is to the rest of the United States (five hundred miles away).

Where in Alaska is it daytime—at night?

Way up in the northern parts of the state, it's light out for twenty hours a day. Just think—in the Land of the Midnight Sun, you could play a baseball game in the middle of the night, in broad daylight! In the winter, though, it's just the opposite—it's dark for twenty hours a day and light for only a few hours.

How can you travel two thousand miles across frozen Alaska without a motor?

By sled-dog! The Iditarod, Alaska's famous annual sled-dog race, is a really tough trek across Alaska that can take twenty days to finish. (If you finish it at all, that is.)

ARIZONA

(AZ)

NICKNAME: THE GRAND CANYON STATE
STATEHOOD: 1912
CAPITAL: PHOENIX
STATE FLOWER: BLOSSOM OF THE SAGUARO CACTUS
STATE BIRD: CACTUS WREN

Saguaro cactus blossom

Cactus wren

Where in Arizona can you travel through two billion years of Earth's history in a single day?

Here's a hint: President Teddy Roosevelt called it "the one great sight every American should see." The answer is the Grand Canyon. The Grand Canyon is 277 miles long, up to 18 miles wide, and more than a mile deep. From the bottom, you can see how the earth was formed by looking at the layers of rock along the canyon's walls.

Who said, "I never do wrong without a cause!"?

Geronimo, an Apache warrior. When white settlers began moving west in the 1850s, Arizona's Apache Indians fought hard to keep their land. One Apache warrior named Geronimo led so many successful attacks that the United States government considered him its chief enemy and offered a $25,000 reward for his capture. After more than thirty years of fighting, Geronimo finally surrendered in 1886 and lived the rest of his life on reservations in Florida and Oklahoma.

Some people say that the cry "Geronimo!" comes from a time when the United States cavalry chased Geronimo to the edge of a cliff. The only way for Geronimo to escape was by jumping off the cliff. The warrior did just that, calling out his name as he fell safely into the river below.

Geronimo?!

ARKANSAS

AR

Mockingbird

True or false: If you find a diamond at Arkansas's Crater of Diamonds State Park, you get to keep it.

True! Crater of Diamonds, near Murfreesboro, is the only diamond mine in North America. The park is open to the public, and its diamonds are finders-keepers. Two or three diamonds are found each day (though they usually aren't the kind you'd use to make jewelry).

Did you know that Arkansas has a fountain of youth?

Well, not really, but Hot Springs National Park does have forty-seven natural springs. Some people believe the springs will make sick people well. You can bathe in the park's bathhouses but not in the springs themselves, since some of them are as hot as 147 degrees!

Apple blossom

How can you find out if you're pronouncing "Arkansas" correctly?

Ask the state legislature. In 1881 it passed a law about how to say the state's name: it's pronounced "ARK-an-saw"—the final *s* is silent.

CALIFORNIA

NICKNAME: THE GOLDEN STATE

STATEHOOD: 1850

CAPITAL: SACRAMENTO

STATE FLOWER: GOLDEN POPPY

STATE BIRD: CALIFORNIA VALLEY QUAIL

CA

California valley quail

Golden poppy

What golden opportunity in 1849 helped California earn its nickname?

Gold was discovered in 1848, and by the next year, many thousands of "forty-niners" came to get rich in the great California Gold Rush of 1849. (Get it? Forty-niners—1849.)

Did you know that California is home to:

• the tallest waterfalls in North America: Yosemite Falls

• the lowest point in the United States, Death Valley, the site of America's highest known temperature—144 degrees.

• the tallest trees on Earth: redwood trees

• the biggest trees on Earth (it would take about twenty-five of your friends holding hands to reach all the way around one tree): giant sequoia trees

Golden State Trivia

Match these California features with the places you'll find them:

1. More TV and movie studios than anywhere else in the world

   A. San Francisco

2. Fossils of plants, birds, and animals stuck in oil and tar since the Ice Age

   B. Silicon Valley

3. The Golden Gate Bridge (which really is red!)

   C. La Brea Tar Pits

4. Tons of computer companies

   D. Hollywood

COLORADO

 CO

NICKNAME: THE CENTENNIAL STATE
STATEHOOD: 1876
CAPITAL: DENVER
STATE FLOWER: ROCKY MOUNTAIN COLUMBINE
STATE BIRD: LARK BUNTING

Rocky Mountain columbine

Lark bunting

What does the Continental Divide divide?

It divides the continent of North America into rivers that run east and empty into the Atlantic Ocean and those that run west and empty into the Pacific Ocean. The Continental Divide runs through the Colorado Rockies.

Why are Coloradans such good sports?

The higher you are above sea level, the thinner the air gets. So, if you throw or hit a ball in Colorado's Rocky Mountains, it will go farther than at lower elevations. All that height is good for sports!

O beautiful for spacious skies,

For amber waves of grain,

For purple mountain majesties

Above the fruited plain!

Did you know that "purple mountain majesties" refers to Colorado's Rocky Mountains? "America the Beautiful" was written by an English professor named Katharine Lee Bates when she picnicked at the top of Colorado's Pikes Peak in 1893. The poem was later set to music.

CONNECTICUT

CT

Mountain laurel

Robin

NICKNAME: THE CONSTITUTION STATE
STATEHOOD: 1788
CAPITAL: HARTFORD
STATE FLOWER: MOUNTAIN LAUREL
STATE BIRD: ROBIN

What Revolutionary War hero born in Connecticut disguised himself as a schoolteacher so he could spy on the British?

Twenty-one-year-old Nathan Hale was hanged by the British in 1776 for spying. He is remembered for the phrase, "I only regret that I have but one life to lose for my country." Connecticut was also home to General Benedict Arnold, America's most infamous Revolutionary War traitor. Arnold was caught plotting to hand over the American fort at West Point to the British. He fled to England before he could be hanged.

A constitution lists the basic laws and rules of a country. The United States Constitution was adopted in 1787.

Why is Connecticut called The Constitution State if the United States Constitution was actually written in Pennsylvania?

When Connecticut's settlers started to form the colony in 1634, they soon adopted the Fundamental Orders, which many people consider the first written American constitution. The orders gave people who voted the right to choose who ran the government.

DELAWARE

Blue hen chicken

NICKNAME: THE FIRST STATE

STATEHOOD: 1787

CAPITAL: DOVER

STATE FLOWER: PEACH BLOSSOM

STATE BIRD: BLUE HEN CHICKEN

⬇ :-)

What did Dela wear to the ball?

Ida ho, Al aska.

Peach blossom

What did Delaware do before any of the other states?

It approved the United States Constitution, thus earning one of its nicknames—the First State. Thomas Jefferson said Delaware was like a diamond, "small, but valuable." (The Diamond State, another of Delaware's nicknames, is indeed small; it's only nine miles wide at its narrowest!)

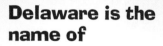

Delaware is the name of

(a) a river

(b) a group of Indians

(c) a state

(d) all of the above

If you answered d, all of the above, you win a Delaware Blue hen! (The Delaware Blue hen was actually a favorite breed of chicken raised in the state more than 200 years ago.) The state was named after the Delaware Indians, only *Delaware* isn't an Indian word at all. British explorers gave this name to the Lenni-Lenape Indian tribe because they lived near the Delaware River, but the river itself was named after Virginia governor Thomas West, Lord De La Warr. (Get it? De-la-ware.) He had never even seen the area.

FLORIDA (FL)

NICKNAME: THE SUNSHINE STATE
STATEHOOD: 1845
CAPITAL: TALLAHASSEE
STATE FLOWER: ORANGE BLOSSOM
STATE BIRD: MOCKINGBIRD

Orange blossom

Mockingbird

Where can Americans go from Cape Canaveral that they can't go from anywhere else in the United States?

Outer space! The John F. Kennedy Space Center is the launching pad for American space missions. From that base:

- astronaut Alan Shepard became the first American in space, in 1961;

- John Glenn became the first American to orbit the Earth, in 1962;

- Neil Armstrong became the first man to walk on the moon, in 1969.

Visitors to the Space Center can sit in a lunar rover, learn how astronauts prepare to go into space, and try on a spacesuit. Blast off!

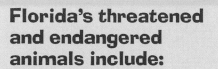

Florida's threatened and endangered animals include:

(a) American crocodiles

(b) bald eagles

(c) manatees

(d) Florida panthers

(e) all of the above

The answer is, sadly, e. Some of the rarest plants and animals in the country live in Florida's Everglades, one of the world's largest swamps, which is itself endangered.

KNOCK, KNOCK!

Who's there?

Orange.

Orange who?

Orange you going to ask about Florida oranges?

Because of the Sunshine State's sunny climate, Florida grows more citrus fruit (oranges, grapefruit, lemons) than any other state.

GEORGIA

NICKNAME:	THE PEACH STATE
STATEHOOD:	1788
CAPITAL:	ATLANTA
STATE FLOWER:	CHEROKEE ROSE
STATE BIRD:	BROWN THRASHER

GA

Brown thrasher

Cherokee rose

If Georgia is old enough to be the fourth state, why are there so few old buildings in Atlanta, its capital?

Poor Atlanta. At the end of the Civil War, Union general William T. Sherman ordered Atlanta to be burned because the Confederates' food and guns were stored there. The city had to be rebuilt from the ground up.

When cola syrup was accidentally mixed with carbonated water and served at Jacobs' Pharmacy in Atlanta in 1886, Coca-Cola was born. Today its secret recipe is known by only two men, who try never to travel together—just in case there's an accident. . . .

Ever heard of goobers?

If you're not from the South, you probably haven't. Here are a few hints: they're what locals call the main ingredient in peanut butter, and they come salted in the shell, honey roasted, and in Snickers bars. Georgia grows more . . . *peanuts* than any other state.

What Georgian was King of the civil rights movement?

The Reverend Dr. Martin Luther King, Jr., was America's most famous civil rights leader. King led nonviolent protests to fight for social and political rights for African Americans and others. In his hometown of Atlanta an eternal flame burns to honor his memory.

18

HAWAII

Yellow hibiscus

(HI)

NICKNAME: THE ALOHA STATE
STATEHOOD: 1959
CAPITAL: HONOLULU
STATE FLOWER: YELLOW HIBISCUS
STATE BIRD: NENE (HAWAIIAN GOOSE)

What is Hawaii, exactly?

Hawaii is both a state and an island. The state of Hawaii is made up of 132 islands, but only eight are big enough to live on. The well-known Hawaiian islands are Maui, Oahu, Kauai, and, of course, Hawaii, called the Big Island. Hawaii is the southernmost place in the United States, and is about two thousand miles from California in the Pacific Ocean.

Nene

How does the island of Hawaii grow larger each year?

Each time Mauna Loa—one of the world's largest active volcanoes—erupts, the lava cools and hardens in the ocean, making the island bigger. This is how all the Hawaiian islands were formed, but the volcanoes on the other islands are no longer active.

The only royal palace in America is Hawaii's Iolani Palace. Hawaii was ruled by kings and queens from 1795 until 1893.

Aloha

Aloha

Aloha

Aloha

Aloha

Aloha

The Hawaiian word *aloha* means:

(a) hello

(b) good-bye

(c) love

(d) friendship

(e) all of the above

The answer is e. What a happy word!

19

IDAHO

 ID

Syringa

Mountain bluebird

NICKNAME:	THE GEM STATE
STATEHOOD:	1890
CAPITAL:	BOISE
STATE FLOWER:	SYRINGA
STATE BIRD:	MOUNTAIN BLUEBIRD

:-)

What peels and chips but doesn't crack?

A potato!

What precious things can you find in Idaho?

Precious stones! The Gem State produces more than eighty different kinds of precious stones, including opals, garnets, sapphires, and rubies.

How do astronauts walk on the moon while keeping their feet on the earth?

NASA astronauts used to practice for missions at Craters of the Moon National Park because the land there looks so much like the land on the moon. The park has many colors of volcanic lava that has hardened into strange, twisted shapes. There are lots of caves and eerie holes in the ground that steam rises out of, too.

"Dice 'em, hash 'em, boil 'em, mash 'em! Idaho! Idaho! Idaho!" What does this Idaho football cheer refer to?

Potatoes, of course! If all the potatoes grown in the state in a year were put end to end, they'd stretch more than two million miles—or to the moon and back eight times! There would be one hundred and twenty potatoes for each person in America. That's a lot of french fries!

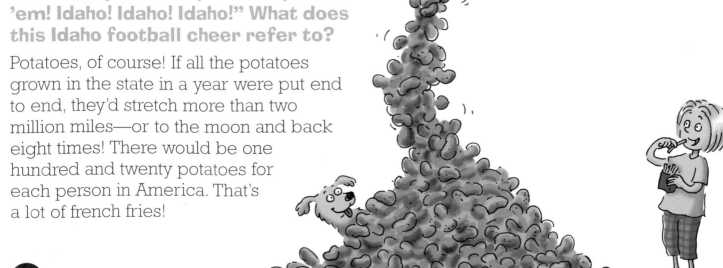

ILLINOIS

IL

Cardinal

What heated up Illinois in 1871?

The great Chicago fire, which rapidly spread through the entire city. The city's wooden houses fed the fire, which burned for more than twenty-four hours and left

Native violet

at least 250 people dead and 100,000 homeless. One good thing came out of the fire, however: Many talented architects helped rebuild the city, which became known for its beautiful and interesting buildings.

What skyscraper is the tallest building in North America?

Chicago's O'Hare airport is the busiest airport in the world. A plane takes off or lands every 23 seconds.

The Sears Tower in Chicago, which is 110 stories high. The tower was the tallest office building in the world when it was built in 1974. Since then, a slightly taller one was built in Kuala Lumpur, Malaysia. You can ride to the top of the Sears Tower in one of the fastest elevators in the world, and on a clear day you can see Wisconsin, Michigan, and Indiana from the top.

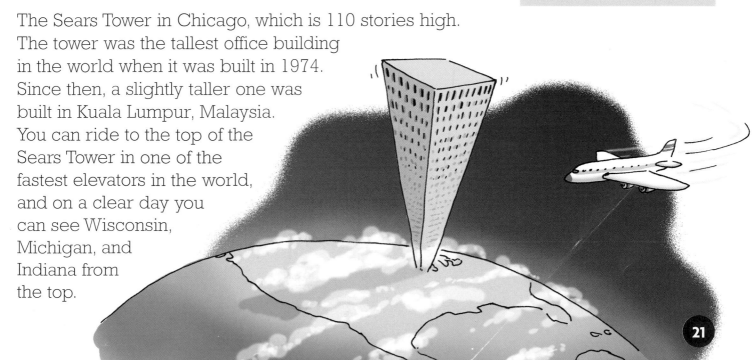

INDIANA

NICKNAME: THE HOOSIER STATE
STATEHOOD: 1816
CAPITAL: INDIANAPOLIS
STATE FLOWER: PEONY
STATE BIRD: CARDINAL

Peony

Cardinal

Garfield creator Jim Davis, basketball star Larry Bird, and singer Michael Jackson are all famous Hoosiers. No one is quite sure why Indiana is called the Hoosier State, but the nickname may come from an early pioneer greeting, "Who'shyer?" meaning "Who's there?" or "How are you?"

Indiana, or *Indian* plus *a*, means "land of Indians." The Illinois, Shawnee, Miami, and other Native American tribes lived here before the settlers arrived.

KNOCK, KNOCK!

Who's there?
Hoosier.
Hoosier who?
Hoosier favorite Hoosier?

If the race car drivers in the Indianapolis 500 drive around the track only 200 times, why is the race called the Indianapolis 500?

The track is 2½ miles long, so the 200 laps make for 500 miles. The drivers go as fast as 237 miles per hour! (That's about three times as fast as your parents drive on the highway.) The race, held each Memorial Day, draws more fans than any other sports event—up to four times as many as the Superbowl.

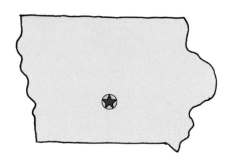

Eastern goldfinch

IOWA

IA

NICKNAME:	THE HAWKEYE STATE
STATEHOOD:	1846
CAPITAL:	DES MOINES
STATE FLOWER:	WILD ROSE
STATE BIRD:	EASTERN GOLDFINCH

If you're driving through Iowa, what will you see out your window?

Farms, farms, and more farms. Farmland makes up about 95 percent of the state. Iowa is also known as the Corn State because it grows more corn than any other state (except sometimes Illinois). Bet it doesn't surprise you that Iowa is home to the biggest popcorn factory in the country.

Wild rose

Ears an interesting fact about Iowa corn: it can grow as high as thirty feet tall! (That's about equal to you and six friends standing on each other's shoulders!)

"I loved my towns, my cornfields, and the home of my people. I fought for it. It is now yours. Keep it as we did. It will produce you good crops."

**Black Hawk,
—Sauk Indian Chief**

Why is Iowa called the Hawkeye State?

Iowa was nicknamed the Hawkeye State in honor of the Indian chief Black Hawk, who was forced to give up his land after the Black Hawk War of 1832. *Iowa* is an Iowa Indian word that means "this is the place" or "the beautiful land."

KANSAS (KS)

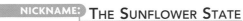

NICKNAME:	THE SUNFLOWER STATE
STATEHOOD:	1861
CAPITAL:	TOPEKA
STATE FLOWER:	SUNFLOWER
STATE BIRD:	WESTERN MEADOWLARK

What took Dorothy and Toto away from their Kansas home?

A tornado. Kansas gets lots of tornadoes. This kind of powerful, swirling storm took Dorothy and her dog to the wonderful Land of Oz. The name "Kansas" comes from the Sioux word *kansa*, meaning "people of the wind."

"The night I flew over the Pacific was a night of stars. They seemed to rise from the sea and hang outside my cockpit window, near enough to touch."

—Amelia Earhart

Sunflower

Western meadowlark

What Kansan set an aviation record?

Airplane pilot Amelia Earhart, who was born in Kansas, was the first woman to fly alone across the Atlantic Ocean, in 1932. In 1937 Earhart mysteriously disappeared over the Pacific Ocean while trying to fly around the world.

(KY)

NICKNAME: THE BLUEGRASS STATE
STATEHOOD: 1792
CAPITAL: FRANKFORT
STATE FLOWER: GOLDENROD
STATE BIRD: KENTUCKY CARDINAL

Kentucky cardinal

Goldenrod

Does the Bluegrass State really have blue grass?

The grass in Kentucky isn't *really* blue, but it does bloom with blue flowers in the spring. The state's thigh-slapping, toe-tapping folk music is also called bluegrass.

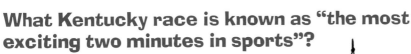

Where in Kentucky can you find eyeless fish and blind beetles?

In the darkest parts of Kentucky's Mammoth Caves, the largest cave system in the whole world. The caves have more than three hundred miles of underground passages, lakes, rivers, and waterfalls (underground waterfalls!)—and that only includes the parts that have been explored.

Most of the United States gold reserve—more than $40 billion—is kept at Kentucky's Fort Knox.

What Kentucky race is known as "the most exciting two minutes in sports"?

The Kentucky Derby, America's oldest yearly horse race, held each May at Louisville's Churchill Downs. Kentucky is famous for its champion racehorses.

LOUISIANA

NICKNAME:	THE PELICAN STATE
STATEHOOD:	1812
CAPITAL:	BATON ROUGE
STATE FLOWER:	MAGNOLIA
STATE BIRD:	EASTERN BROWN PELICAN

Eastern brown pelican

Magnolia

Why is the Pelican State also called the Sportsman's Paradise?

Louisiana is home to lots of pelicans. Pelicans love to catch fish, and Louisiana is a great place for sportsmen to do the same. With the Mississippi River, the Gulf of Mexico, and all of the state's swamps and bayous (*BI-yooz*), Louisiana makes more money from fishing than any other state. The Fisherman's Paradise exports shrimp, oysters, and frogs, and much of the world's crayfish.

What musician made New Orleans famous as "the cradle of jazz"?

Jazz, a kind of music that combines music from Africa and the American South, started in New Orleans in the early 1900s. Around the same time, a young musician named Louis Armstrong was singing for pennies on the streets and playing a guitar he had made out of a cigar box. Armstrong eventually helped make jazz famous with his trumpet playing and unique singing voice.

A bayou is what Louisianans call a stream or creek. Bayous are often marshy, shallow, and full of fish and wild animals to hunt.

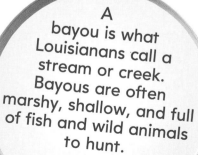

26

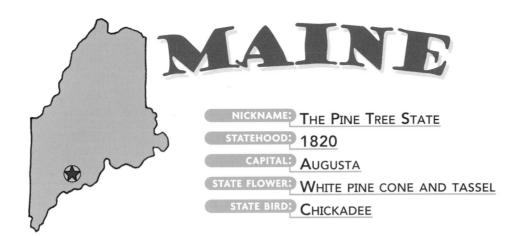

MAINE

NICKNAME:	THE PINE TREE STATE
STATEHOOD:	1820
CAPITAL:	AUGUSTA
STATE FLOWER:	WHITE PINE CONE AND TASSEL
STATE BIRD:	CHICKADEE

White pine cone and tassel

(ME)

Strain your brain on Maine: Which of the following are true?

(a) It's the only state whose name has only one syllable.

(b) Lions with thick, bushy *manes* live in the state.

(c) French explorers might have named it after a region in France called *Mayne*.

(d) The state is the *main* place in America for lighthouses, lobster, and wild blueberries.

If you guessed a, c, and d, you're right! As for the lions . . . you'll have to head to Africa, or to the zoo!

Chickadee

If you live in West Quoddy Head, Maine, what do you get to do before anyone else in the United States, every single day of every year?

See the sun rise! West Quoddy Head is farther east than any other place on the East Coast of the United States. Now, quick: Do you remember which state is the farthest south? If not, unscramble these letters—AIWHAI—or turn to page 19 to find out!

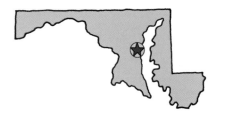

MARYLAND

NICKNAME:	THE OLD LINE STATE
STATEHOOD:	1788
CAPITAL:	ANNAPOLIS
STATE FLOWER:	BLACK-EYED SUSAN
STATE BIRD:	BALTIMORE ORIOLE

Baltimore oriole

Black-eyed Susan

What's the key to remembering who wrote our National Anthem?

The fact that the poet's last name is Key! In 1814 Francis Scott Key wrote "The Star-Spangled Banner." He was inspired by a twenty-five-hour battle between the Americans and the British during the War of 1812. As Key watched the battle at Fort McHenry from a sailboat in Baltimore harbor, he kept his eye out for the American flag. He knew that as long as the Stars and Stripes flew, the Americans had not been defeated. When the battle was over, he wrote his famous words on the back of a letter he happened to have in his pocket. The poem, later set to music, was to become the national anthem of the United States.

Was the Underground Railroad the first subway system?

It sure sounds like it, but the Underground Railroad was really a series of houses and other safe places for slaves who were running away to freedom before the Civil War. Abolitionists (people who were against slavery) helped the slaves move north from one station along the "railroad" to another, usually at night. Harriet Tubman, herself an escaped slave who grew up in Maryland, became one of the most famous "conductors" of the Underground Railroad and helped at least three hundred other slaves escape.

"I was a conductor on the Underground Railroad for eight years, and I can say what most conductors can't say—I never ran my train off the track and I never lost a passenger."

—Abolitionist Harriet Tubman

MASSACHUSETTS

(MA)

NICKNAME:	THE BAY STATE
STATEHOOD:	1788
CAPITAL:	BOSTON
STATE FLOWER:	MAYFLOWER
STATE BIRD:	CHICKADEE

Mayflower

Chickadee

Was Massachusetts the site of the first British colony in America?

It seems like it should be, because we learn so much about the Pilgrims and their first Thanksgiving. But Plymouth, where the Pilgrims landed, was actually the second permanent British colony in America. Jamestown, Virginia, was the first, in 1607.

Where was Paul Revere going on his famous midnight ride?

On April 18, 1775, the night before the first battles of the American Revolution, Paul Revere left Boston on horseback for Lexington and Concord. It's a good thing he wasn't the only rider carrying the message that the British were coming, because Revere was captured just as he left Lexington. One of the other patriots, Samuel Prescott, made it to Concord.

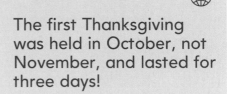

The first Thanksgiving was held in October, not November, and lasted for three days!

Why is Massachusetts the best place for little women to eat green eggs and ham?

Because both Louisa May Alcott, author of *Little Women*, and Theodor Geisel (better known as Dr. Seuss!) were born here. Other famous authors include Emily Dickinson, Ralph Waldo Emerson, and Edgar Allan Poe.

29

MICHIGAN

Robin

Apple blossom

NICKNAME:	THE WOLVERINE STATE
STATEHOOD:	1837
CAPITAL:	LANSING
STATE FLOWER:	APPLE BLOSSOM
STATE BIRD:	ROBIN

MI

Michigan is broken into two separate pieces of land. Its Upper and Lower Peninsulas touch four of the five Great Lakes: Erie, Huron, Michigan, and Superior. With all the nooks and crannies, this gives the state a shoreline of 3,100 miles! The name "Michigan" comes from two Chippewa Indian words, *mici* and *gama*, that together mean "great water."

What product of Detroit is this 1901 advertisement promoting?

"Travels rough roads smoothly. A child can operate it safely. Speed up to 25 miles per hour without fear of breakdown. Goes 40 miles on one gallon of gasoline."

A "horseless carriage" (a car). Detroit is often called "Motor City" or "Motortown" because it makes more cars than any other city in the world.

How did Motown music get its name?

Detroit is also famous for its music, "Motown" (short for Motortown), which combines pop and black gospel music. If you've ever heard the song "Stop! In the Name of Love" by the Supremes, then you know what Motown sounds like.

If you want to remember the names of the five Great Lakes, just remember the word HOMES, for: **H**uron, **O**ntario, **M**ichigan, **E**rie, **S**uperior.

MINNESOTA

MN

NICKNAME: THE LAND OF **10,000** LAKES
STATEHOOD: 1858
CAPITAL: ST. PAUL
STATE FLOWER: PINK AND WHITE LADY'S SLIPPER
STATE BIRD: COMMON LOON

Common loon

Pink and white lady's slipper

Are there really 10,000 lakes in Minnesota?

Actually, there are at least 15,000, and maybe more than 22,000. There are so many lakes in Minnesota that people ran out of names and started using old names over again! There are 201 Mud Lakes, 154 Long Lakes, 123 Rice Lakes, and 83 Bass Lakes.

:-)

Why shouldn't you tell a joke while ice fishing?

The ice might crack up!

What Minnesotan was so big that he used a pine tree to brush his beard?

Of all tall-tale heroes, Paul Bunyan was probably the tallest. In the 1800s loggers told stories about the huge imaginary lumberjack who lived in Minnesota with his blue ox, Babe. Legend has it that each of Paul's enormous footprints became one of Minnesota's lakes.

MISSISSIPPI

NICKNAME: THE MAGNOLIA STATE
STATEHOOD: 1817
CAPITAL: JACKSON
STATE FLOWER: MAGNOLIA
STATE BIRD: MOCKINGBIRD

(MS)

Mockingbird

Magnolia

:-)
What has four eyes but can't see?

ıddıssıssıW

Of the ten states that border the Mississippi River, why was the state of Mississippi the one to be named after it?

No other state had taken the name yet! The name of this state, and the largest river in America, most likely comes from two Chippewa Indian words, *mici* and *zibi*, meaning "father of the waters." The rich, dark soil deposited by the river is some of the best in the world for growing crops.

What do you get when you combine a marionette and a puppet?

Grover, Oscar the Grouch, Miss Piggy, Kermit the Frog—Muppets! The Muppets' creator, Jim Henson, grew up in Leland and named Kermit after one of his childhood friends.

MISSOURI

NICKNAME: THE SHOW ME STATE
STATEHOOD: 1821
CAPITAL: JEFFERSON CITY
STATE FLOWER: HAWTHORN
STATE BIRD: BLUEBIRD

MO

Bluebird

Hawthorn

"Wanted—young, skinny, wiry fellows not over 18. Must be expert riders, willing to risk death daily. Orphans preferred. Wages $25 a week."

If you answered this ad from an 1860 Missouri newspaper, you'd be hoping to ride for the Pony Express, an early mail service that carried letters from St. Joseph, Missouri, to Sacramento, California, before America's cross-country telegraph lines were connected.

Brave riders rode on horseback at top speed, even in snow or through the desert, to cover the two thousand miles in just ten days.

Missouri is one of only two states to border eight other states: Iowa, Illinois, Kentucky, Tennessee, Arkansas, Oklahoma, Kansas, and Nebraska. Which of these states also touches eight states? Hint: It's the only one that has more letters in its name than the number of states it touches.

Answer: Tennessee

"There comes a time in every rightly constructed boy's life when he has a raging desire to go somewhere and dig for hidden treasure."

—*The Adventures of Tom Sawyer*

In Mark Twain's book, Tom and his friend Huck Finn decide to become pirates on the Mississippi River. Twain (whose real name was Samuel Langhorne Clemens) grew up in Hannibal and later was a riverboat pilot on the Mississippi.

MONTANA

NICKNAME:	THE TREASURE STATE
STATEHOOD:	1889
CAPITAL:	HELENA
STATE FLOWER:	BITTERROOT
STATE BIRD:	WESTERN MEADOWLARK

MT

Western meadowlark

Bitterroot

Have pirates been hiding out in Montana?

Without a coast, Montana hasn't been visited by any pirates, but the state does have buried treasure of another kind. Gold, silver, copper, and zinc are all mined in the Treasure State, which also produces more sapphires than any other state.

Who was left standing at Custer's Last Stand?

The Sioux and Cheyenne warriors, led by Crazy Horse. Custer's Last Stand, also known as the Battle of Little Bighorn, in 1876 was the Indians' last and largest victory during the Plains Indian Wars. Lieutenant Colonel George A. Custer thought he was so powerful that he paid no attention to warnings that his army would be greatly outnumbered. In the space of just one hour, Custer and all his men lost their lives. His defeat embarrassed and angered the American government, causing it to fight the Indians even harder.

Montana, called Big Sky Country, has set aside twenty-five million acres of land on which elk, grizzly bears, mountain lions, and buffalo are free to roam. The state also has lots of sheep and cattle ranches: In Montana, cows outnumber people by about three to one.

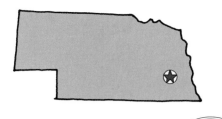

NEBRASKA

(NE)

Goldenrod

NICKNAME: THE CORNHUSKER STATE
STATEHOOD: 1867
CAPITAL: LINCOLN
STATE FLOWER: GOLDENROD
STATE BIRD: WESTERN MEADOWLARK

Why were Nebraska's first settlers called "sodbusters"?

There may not have been many trees in Nebraska when the first settlers arrived, but there *was* a lot of grass. So settlers made their houses out of sod, or thin layers of dirt and grass, which they cut, or "busted," into blocks.

What national holiday has its roots in Nebraska?

Arbor Day, a holiday for planting trees, was started in 1872 in then almost treeless Nebraska by a man named J. Sterling Morton. Morton knew that trees would enable people to build houses and barns, help protect people from floods and blizzards, and make the soil more fertile. The Nebraska National Forest is the only national forest planted solely by people.

Nebraska is the only state to take its nickname from a college mascot, the University of Nebraska's Cornhusker. (The university took the name from the state's main agricultural product and from the cornhusking contests farmers used to hold.)

Western meadowlark

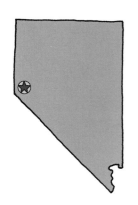

NEVADA

NV

NICKNAME: THE SILVER STATE
STATEHOOD: 1864
CAPITAL: CARSON CITY
STATE FLOWER: SAGEBRUSH
STATE BIRD: MOUNTAIN BLUEBIRD

Sagebrush

Mountain bluebird

To build Nevada's Hoover Dam, concrete was poured continually for:

(a) one day

(c) two years

(b) three months

(d) ten years

The answer is c: two years! The 726-foot-high Hoover Dam gives water to local farms and electricity to Nevada, Arizona, and southern California. The dam created Lake Mead, the largest man-made lake in the United States and one of the largest in the world.

What Nevada city am I?

- With all my neon lights and air-conditioning, I have the highest electric bills per person in America.

- I am the live entertainment capital of the world.

- Four hundred couples get married in me every day.

- I am home to more than fifty casinos, where people try their luck at cards, dice, and other games of chance.

I'm Las Vegas!

NEW HAMPSHIRE

(NH)

NICKNAME: THE GRANITE STATE
STATEHOOD: 1788
CAPITAL: CONCORD
STATE FLOWER: PURPLE LILAC
STATE BIRD: PURPLE FINCH

Purple finch

Purple lilac

Did you know it?
New Hampshire's a prizewinning poet!

Well, the Pulitzer Prize for poetry didn't actually go to the state, it went to Robert Frost for his book called *New Hampshire*. Robert Frost was born in San Francisco but later settled on a farm in New Hampshire. Frost is famous for his many poems about New England and its people. In a poem called "New Hampshire," Frost says the state is one of the two best in America. (The other being New Hampshire's next-door neighbor, Vermont, where he was living at the time!)

Why is New Hampshire sometimes known as the "state that made the nation"?

Nine of the original thirteen colonies needed to approve the Constitution for the United States to become a nation. New Hampshire was the ninth to do so. New Hampshirites also were the first colonists to declare their independence from England: they formed their own government in January 1776—six months before the Declaration of Independence was signed!

The Library of Congress in Washington, D.C., is made from New Hampshire's granite, a hard gray rock that lies under much of the state.

If you go to Mount Washington, hold on to your hat! A wind of 231 miles per hour, the strongest wind ever recorded in the United States, blew across it in 1934.

37

NEW JERSEY

NICKNAME:	THE GARDEN STATE
STATEHOOD:	1787
CAPITAL:	TRENTON
STATE FLOWER:	PURPLE VIOLET
STATE BIRD:	EASTERN GOLDFINCH

NJ

Eastern goldfinch

Purple violet

If New Jersey has so many smokestacks and factories, why is it called the Garden State?

New Jersey does have lots of factories and more people per square mile than any other state, but the Garden State also has sandy beaches and beautiful farmland. During the American Revolution, New Jersey farms provided much of the food the soldiers needed to win the war. Today the state grows food for nearby Philadelphia and New York City.

What famous inventor, known as the "Wizard of Menlo Park," had only three months of formal schooling?

Thomas Edison invented the movie camera, the electric lightbulb, the phonograph, even wax paper—all told, over 1,093 inventions in his lifetime. When Edison opened his factory in Menlo Park in 1876, he said it would produce "a minor invention every ten days and a big thing every six months or so." And it did!

If you're strolling down Atlantic Avenue, the Boardwalk, and Park Place, are you in a life-sized game of Monopoly?

No, you're in Atlantic City. The spaces of the board game Monopoly are named after its streets.

NEW MEXICO

(NM)

NICKNAME: THE LAND OF ENCHANTMENT
STATEHOOD: 1912
CAPITAL: SANTA FE
STATE FLOWER: YUCCA
STATE BIRD: ROADRUNNER

Yucca

Roadrunner

If New Mexico is "new," how can it be so old?

Spanish explorers named the area New Mexico way back in 1540, when they first came north from Mexico. In many parts of the state, you can see pottery with designs that can be traced back more than two thousand years, to the Anasazi Indians.

Why do many buildings in New Mexico look different from those in other states?

Many buildings in New Mexico are made of *adobe* bricks, or blocks of clay and straw that have been dried in the sun. People who live in the desert have built adobe houses for hundreds of years because these houses stay cool in the heat, and wood was not available. In Taos you can find one of New Mexico's oldest adobe *pueblos*, or villages, built more than 700 years ago. Today, the state is known for its unique mix of Indian, Spanish, and American traditions.

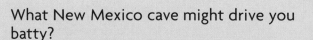

What New Mexico cave might drive you batty?

Carlsbad Caverns in southeastern New Mexico are the deepest limestone caves in the world. Every night, thousands of bats fly out of the caves and return before morning.

NEW YORK

NICKNAME:	THE EMPIRE STATE
STATEHOOD:	1788
CAPITAL:	ALBANY
STATE FLOWER:	ROSE
STATE BIRD:	BLUEBIRD

Did all of New York's Manhattan Island really cost just $24?

Peter Minuit, the leader of the Dutch colony of New Amsterdam, bought Manhattan in 1626 from the Lenape Indians for $24 worth of beads, cloth, and hatchets. Today that sum would be worth about $480—which still makes the purchase a bargain! The British renamed New Amsterdam New York in 1664, for the Duke of York, Britain's future king.

I'm big, I'm green, I'm America's Welcome Queen. Who am I?

The Statue of Liberty, in New York harbor, which greeted people as they arrived by boat to settle in the United States, is technically in New Jersey. The statue, a gift from France, is still a reminder of hope and freedom—the reasons many people move to America. Today you can climb 354 steps inside her to reach the crown.

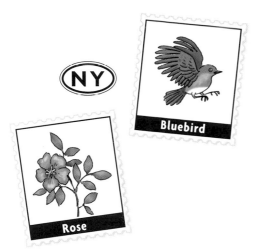

Bluebird

Rose

The first stop for people entering New York harbor was Ellis Island. It was called the "Gateway to the New World" because twelve million people who wanted to move to the United States stopped at the island between 1892 and 1954. Did you know that chances are one in three that you have a relative who stopped at Ellis Island?

Beautiful Niagara Falls are actually two waterfalls. One's in New York, and the other is in Canada. Niagara Falls has inspired people to do some crazy things:

- A man named Sam Patch dove over not once, but twice, in the late 1820s.

- Schoolteacher Annie Taylor became the first to go over the falls in a barrel, in 1901. She lived, but others who tried later were not as lucky.

- French daredevil Charles Blondin crossed the falls many times on his tightrope in 1859 and 1860. Once he pushed a stove along in a wheelbarrow and halfway across cooked himself an omelet!

NORTH CAROLINA

NC

NICKNAME:	THE TAR HEEL STATE
STATEHOOD:	1789
CAPITAL:	RALEIGH
STATE FLOWER:	DOGWOOD
STATE BIRD:	CARDINAL

Cardinal

Dogwood

So what's a Tar Heel, anyway?

North Carolina's pine trees make a lot of tar—and tar, of course, is very sticky. Legend has it that during the Civil War, North Carolina soldiers stood as bravely in battle as if they had tar on their heels.

What two brothers had the Wright stuff?

Orville and Wilbur Wright brought their flying machine to Kitty Hawk, North Carolina, on December 17, 1903, because the National Weather Service said the spot was one of the windiest in North America—and they needed wind to get their airplane off the ground. The first successful powered airplane flight lasted twelve seconds, and the craft traveled about half a football field.

The first English colony in America was started on North Carolina's Roanoke Island in 1587. Just a few years after the colony was settled, though, its people mysteriously disappeared. Almost no trace of the settlers from the "Lost Colony" was found, not even skeletons.

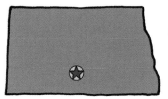

NORTH DAKOTA

NICKNAME:	THE FLICKERTAIL STATE
STATEHOOD:	1889
CAPITAL:	BISMARCK
STATE FLOWER:	WILD PRAIRIE ROSE
STATE BIRD:	WESTERN MEADOWLARK

Western meadowlark

Wild prairie rose

Why do North and South Dakota share the same name?

The two states together were once the Dakota Territory, named for a nation of Oglala, Lakota, Teton, and other Indians who called themselves Dakota, or "league of friends." The territory was made into two states because it was so large.

Who was Sacagawea?

In 1804, Meriwether Lewis and William Clark set out to explore the Louisiana Territory. Near their winter camp in Washburn, a Shoshone Indian teenager named Sacagawea joined them. (You can see her picture on the gold-colored dollar coin.) She spoke English because she had once been captured and sold to a Canadian fur trapper. Without her help as a guide and interpreter, it is doubtful that Lewis and Clark would have reached the Pacific Ocean.

"I would never have been president if it had not been for my experiences in North Dakota."
—Theodore Roosevelt

President Teddy Roosevelt spent three years on a ranch in North Dakota in the 1880s. Roosevelt is the only president to have a national park, Theodore Roosevelt National Park, in southwest North Dakota, named after him.

 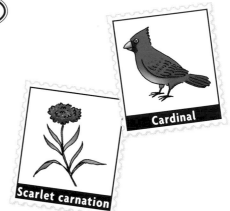

Cardinal

Scarlet carnation

How many United States presidents were born in Ohio?

Ohio sometimes is called the Mother of Modern Presidents because seven American presidents, all of whom served after the Civil War, were born there: Ulysses S. Grant, Rutherford B. Hayes, James Garfield, Benjamin Harrison, William McKinley, William Howard Taft, and Warren G. Harding.

:-)

What state is round at the ends and high in the middle?

¡O-IH-O

Why does Ohio have oodles of apple orchards?

John Chapman, better known as Johnny Appleseed, was born in Massachusetts in 1774, but he spent most of his life planting apple trees in the Ohio River valley. He gave apple seeds and seedlings to everyone he met. He loved apples, apple trees, and animals, and was a friend of the Indians. Folklore says he traveled barefoot and wore a tin pot as a hat and a coffee sack as a shirt.

OKLAHOMA

Mistletoe

Scissortailed flycatcher

OK

NICKNAME: THE SOONER STATE
STATEHOOD: 1907
CAPITAL: OKLAHOMA CITY
STATE FLOWER: MISTLETOE
STATE BIRD: SCISSORTAILED FLYCATCHER

I'm gooey, black, and will make you rich, and I'm called Oklahoma's "black gold." What am I?

Oil! Oklahoma has so much oil underground that people have discovered oil in their backyards. There's even an oil well on the lawn of the state capitol!

Why are there more languages spoken in Oklahoma than in all of Europe?

Oklahoma is home to at least fifty-five Indian nations, each of which has its own language or dialect. Each tribe controls its own government, schools, and land. The name "Oklahoma" comes from two Choctaw Indian words: *humma* and *okla*, meaning "red people."

Were some of Oklahoma's first white settlers a little bit naughty?

At noon on April 22, 1889, the United States opened the Oklahoma Territory for settlement. A gun was fired to start the land rush . . . but some eager settlers "jumped the gun" and claimed their land early. The Sooner State gets its name from the pioneers who thought they would get better land if they got there "sooner."

Most of the Indian tribes who now live in Oklahoma were forced to walk there by the United States government during the mid-1800s. The journey became known as the Trail of Tears because so many died along the way.

OREGON

Western meadowlark

OR

Were pioneers on the Oregon Trail really headed for Oregon?

The Oregon Trail was a two-thousand-mile route that pioneers followed to Oregon and other places in the West in the 1840s to the 1860s. In some places along the trail, you can still see the tracks made by the thousands of covered wagons that traveled along it more than 150 years ago.

Oregon grape

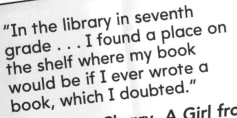

"In the library in seventh grade . . . I found a place on the shelf where my book would be if I ever wrote a book, which I doubted."

—Beverly Cleary, A Girl from Yamhill: A Memoir

What Oregon-born author overcame her doubts and went on to create Ramona Quimby?

Beverly Cleary's stories about Ramona Quimby, Ramona's older sister, Beezus, and their neighbor, Henry Huggins, take place just outside the city of Portland.

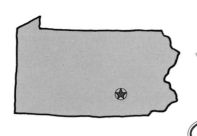

PENNSYLVANIA

PA

Mountain laurel

NICKNAME:	THE KEYSTONE STATE
STATEHOOD:	1787
CAPITAL:	HARRISBURG
STATE FLOWER:	MOUNTAIN LAUREL
STATE BIRD:	RUFFLED GROUSE

Ruffled grouse

What is a keystone anyway?

A keystone is the stone that holds an arch together. Pennsylvania is called the Keystone State. It sat right in the middle of the colonies, and both the Declaration of Independence and the U.S. Constitution were signed at the Pennsylvania State House in Philadelphia.

You turkey!

Ben Franklin was one of America's most famous writers, leaders, and scientists. He created Philadelphia's first fire department, Pennsylvania's first university and public hospital, and the nation's first public library. But when it came to fowl, his ideas were foul! Ben wanted to make the wild turkey the national symbol, because it lived only in America and Ben thought it acted nobly. Thank goodness the bald eagle was chosen instead!

Ben Franklin started a magazine called *Poor Richard's Almanac*, which included famous Franklin sayings, such as:

"Early to bed, and early to rise, makes a man healthy, wealthy, and wise."

"Fish and visitors smell in three days."

"Three may keep a secret if two are dead."

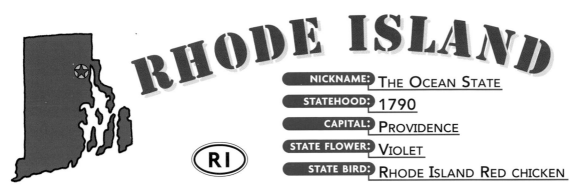

RHODE ISLAND

RI

NICKNAME:	THE OCEAN STATE
STATEHOOD:	1790
CAPITAL:	PROVIDENCE
STATE FLOWER:	VIOLET
STATE BIRD:	RHODE ISLAND RED CHICKEN

Just how small is "Little Rhody"?

It's only forty-eight miles long and thirty-seven miles wide. Do you remember how many times Rhode Island could fit inside Alaska? See page 9 for the answer! It's funny that the smallest state in the nation has the longest official name: The State of Rhode Island and Providence Plantations.

Where is the founder of Rhode Island buried?

No one knows! Rhode Island settlers were grateful for Roger Williams, who founded Rhode Island as the first colony where people could practice any religion freely. Williams and his wife were first buried on their farm in Providence. But when admiring Rhode Islanders decided to dig up the graves and give them a fancier place to rest, the graves were empty!

If you just arrived in Rhode Island, is it more likely that you rode in a car or rowed a boat to get there?

Violet

Since Rhode Island isn't really an island, you probably came by car. Rhode Island got its name from just one of the islands that is now part of the state of Rhode Island. (Today, the Ocean State is made up of thirty-six islands and one mainland.) And as for the "Rhode"? In 1524, Italian explorer Giovanni da Verrazzano said the island was about the same size as the Greek island of Rhodes. "Rhode" may also have come from the Dutch explorer Adriaen Block, who called the island *Roodt*, or red, because of its red soil.

Rhode Island Red

SOUTH CAROLINA

NICKNAME: THE PALMETTO STATE
STATEHOOD: 1788
CAPITAL: COLUMBIA
STATE FLOWER: CAROLINA JESSAMINE
STATE BIRD: CAROLINA WREN

SC

Carolina jessamine

Carolina wren

Who was Caroline, and why does she get two states named after her?

Believe it or not, there was no Caroline at all. "Carolina" is the Latin form of "Charles." Carolina (North and South were originally just one state) was named to honor England's Kings Charles I and Charles II and France's King Charles IX.

Venus's-flytraps, wild plants that eat meat, grow only in North and South Carolina.

What are palmettos, and why is South Carolina so fond of them?

Palmettos are just what they sound like—baby palm trees with fan-shaped leaves. The trees helped South Carolina soldiers win one of the first battles of the Revolutionary War, which they fought from a fort built with soft palmetto logs. The British cannonballs sank right into the spongy wood!

49

SOUTH DAKOTA

NICKNAME:	THE COYOTE STATE
STATEHOOD:	1889
CAPITAL:	PIERRE
STATE FLOWER:	PASQUEFLOWER
STATE BIRD:	CHINESE RING-NECKED PHEASANT

Pasqueflower

SD

Thousands of years ago you would have found small three-toed horses, sabre-toothed tigers, and camels in the Badlands.

What's so bad about the Badlands?

The Badlands are a region in South Dakota of steep cliffs and strange, spooky rock formations, carved by thousands of years of exposure to wind and water, and extreme temperatures. The Sioux Indians called the area "land bad" because it was so hard to live on and travel across. But some people think the layers of pink, orange, gold, green, blue, silver, gray, and brown rocks are beautiful.

Over 13 feet high and 42 feet long, "Sue" might be the biggest, meanest, and oldest known inhabitant of South Dakota. This famous *Tyrannosaurus rex* skeleton has been around for about 60 million years.

The men of Mount Rushmore: Who doesn't belong?

George Washington

Thomas Jefferson

Gutzon Borglum

Teddy Roosevelt

Abraham Lincoln

All these men belong, but Gutzon Borglum's face is not on the mountain. He designed South Dakota's Mount Rushmore, one of the largest stone carvings in the world. Each of the sixty-foot-tall presidents' heads was carved using dynamite and jackhammers.

Chinese ring-necked pheasant

No wonder the project, started in 1927, took workers fourteen years to complete—even though they were *dynamite* sculptors!

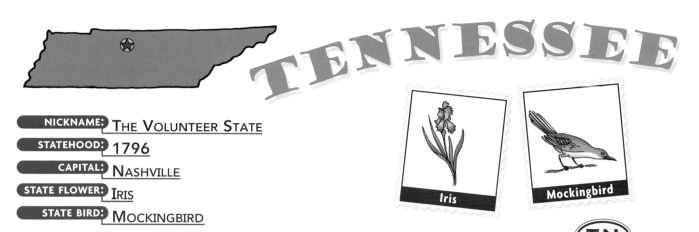

TENNESSEE

NICKNAME: THE VOLUNTEER STATE
STATEHOOD: 1796
CAPITAL: NASHVILLE
STATE FLOWER: IRIS
STATE BIRD: MOCKINGBIRD

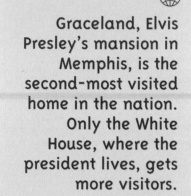

Iris

Mockingbird

TN

Is Tennessee called the Volunteer State because its residents do lots of community service?

Not really. Tennessee has been known as the Volunteer State since 1847, when the United States was fighting the Mexican War. The government asked Tennessee for three thousand volunteer soldiers, and thirty thousand joined.

Yee-haw! What Tennessee city is the home of country music?

Nashville is known as "Music City, USA." A country music radio show called *The Grand Ole Opry* started in Nashville in the 1920s. It helped make country music popular. *The Opry* is the longest-running live radio show in the world.

Graceland, Elvis Presley's mansion in Memphis, is the second-most visited home in the nation. Only the White House, where the president lives, gets more visitors.

What Tennessee frontiersman was famous for wearing a coonskin cap?

Frontier settler Davy Crockett won hundreds of shooting contests as a young man. He later served in the army in the early 1800s and was then elected to Congress three times. Crockett said, "I leave this rule for others when I'm dead: Be always sure you're right—then go ahead."

TEXAS

NICKNAME: THE LONE STAR STATE
STATEHOOD: 1845
CAPITAL: AUSTIN
STATE FLOWER: BLUEBONNET
STATE BIRD: MOCKINGBIRD

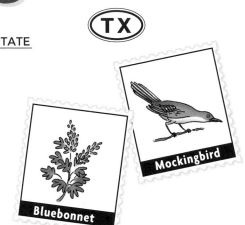

TX

Bluebonnet

Mockingbird

Why is it best if you don't mess with Texas?

Texas has always been fiercely independent—not the kind of state you want to mess with! In fact, Texas was once its own country, with its own flag, which had one star on it to symbolize Texas alone. (That's why it's called the Lone Star State.) During the Texas Revolution in the 1830s, when Texas won its independence from Mexico, 187 volunteers defended a fort known as the Alamo for thirteen days. All the Texans at the fort were killed, but Texas leader Sam Houston went on to win the revolution by inspiring his soldiers with the battle cry, "Remember the Alamo!"

True or false: A nodding donkey is an animal you'll find in a Texas zoo.

False—but you will find them in Texas oil fields. People drill for oil all over Texas with pumps called "nodding donkeys." The pumps are called this because that's what they look like as they pump up and down, bringing oil up to the surface.

Do all Texans wear cowboy boots and ten-gallon hats?

Not today, but many did more than a hundred years ago when cowboys rode horses to herd cattle north from Texas. They also wore:

- spurs, to make their horses go faster;
- chaps, to protect their legs from rain, thorns, and cattle horns;
- bandannas, to keep dust off their faces;
- Stetsons, the most popular kind of cowboy hat, to keep the sun off their heads.

Texas is so big that different parts of the state have completely different climates—it could be snowing in the north and blazing hot in the south on the same day!

Did you know that one out of every three cowboys was either African American or Mexican?

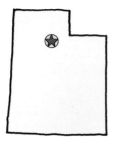

UTAH

NICKNAME:	THE BEEHIVE STATE
STATEHOOD:	1896
CAPITAL:	SALT LAKE CITY
STATE FLOWER:	SEGO LILY
STATE BIRD:	SEAGULL

UT

Sego lily

Seagull

Will you get lots of bee stings in the Beehive State?

No. Utah is nicknamed the Beehive State not for bees, but in honor of the Mormons, a religious group that was the state's first white settlers. The Mormons believe in working industriously and living together in close communities the same way bees do. On the very first day they arrived in 1847, they got to work plowing and making ditches for water so they could farm Utah's dry land.

Why is it so hard to drown in Utah's Great Salt Lake?

The water of the Great Salt Lake is so salty that it's almost impossible to sink in it. The water is four times as salty as ocean water, which makes it very good for floating.

- Utah is home to the biggest dinosaur footprints in the world, made by a hadrosaurid (duckbill) dinosaur.
- Utah is home to more kids under the age of ten than any other state as a percentage of the population.
- A golden spike was hammered into the ground in 1869 at Utah's Golden Spike National Historic Site, where railroads connecting the country's east and west sides first met.

VERMONT

NICKNAME: THE GREEN MOUNTAIN STATE
STATEHOOD: 1791
CAPITAL: MONTPELIER
STATE FLOWER: RED CLOVER
STATE BIRD: HERMIT THRUSH

VT

Red clover

Hermit thrush

The National Rotten Sneaker Championship is held in Montpelier. People enter old sneakers, and winners get a new pair of shoes and a can of Dr. Scholl's foot powder. Being a judge for that contest stinks!

The Green Mountain State is the perfect nickname for Vermont because:

a) The name "Vermont" comes from the French *vert mont*, which means "green mountain."

b) Vermont has lots of green forests and beautiful mountains.

c) It's the name of Ben & Jerry's pistachio ice cream.

They're all true. . . . Well, except the one about the ice cream. Both forests and mountains are important to the Green Mountain State. Tourists come to see Vermont's forests change colors in the fall and to go downhill skiing in the winter.

How many trees does it take to make one gallon of maple syrup?

Four trees' worth (forty gallons) of sugar maple sap must be boiled down to make just one gallon of maple syrup. Vermont makes more maple syrup than any other state.

VIRGINIA

NICKNAME:	THE OLD DOMINION
STATEHOOD:	1788
CAPITAL:	RICHMOND
STATE FLOWER:	FLOWERING DOGWOOD
STATE BIRD:	CARDINAL

Cardinal

Flowering dogwood

Why is Virginia called both a mother and a father?

Virginia is the Mother of Presidents, because eight presidents were born there: George Washington, Thomas Jefferson, James Madison, James Monroe, William Henry Harrison, John Tyler, Zachary Taylor, and Woodrow Wilson. The state is the Father of States, because eight other states were made from the land that used to be part of Virginia: Illinois, Indiana, Kentucky, Michigan, Minnesota, Ohio, West Virginia, and Wisconsin.

Did Pocahontas really save John Smith's life?

Maybe. Captain John Smith was the leader of Jamestown, the first permanent English settlement in America, founded in 1607. According to Smith, when he was captured by the powerful Indian leader Powhatan, Powhatan's eleven-year-old daughter, Pocahontas, threw herself on Smith so he wouldn't be killed. No one knows if the story is actually true, but even if it was made up, it had a powerful effect on establishing peace between the Indians and the colonists.

Match the Founding Father below with one of his claims to fame:

1. He said, "Give me liberty, or give me death!" at the Virginia Convention in 1775.

2. He was ambassador to France and served the first french fries in America at his Virginia home.

3. Washington, D.C., was built near his birthplace in northern Virginia to honor him.

A. George Washington

B. Patrick Henry

C. Thomas Jefferson

Answers: 1-B 2-C 3-A

56

WASHINGTON

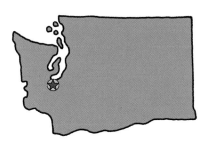

Willow goldfinch

Rhododendron

NICKNAME: THE CHINOOK STATE
STATEHOOD: 1889
CAPITAL: OLYMPIA
STATE FLOWER: RHODODENDRON
STATE BIRD: WILLOW GOLDFINCH

WA

Now Entering
WASHINGTON
STATE

Washington
is the only state
named for a
president.

Why is half of Washington wet and the other half dry?

The Chinook State was named both for the Chinook Indian tribe that lived there and for a pair of winds that affect the state's weather. The winds push rain clouds from west to east. But halfway across the state, they're stopped by the Cascade Mountains. Because the wind and clouds can't get past the peaks to the east side, much more rain falls on the west side of the Cascades.

What famous Washington landmark blew its top?

The explosion of Washington's Mount St. Helens in 1980 was the largest volcanic eruption people have recorded in America. Ash turned the sky black while mud and lava flattened trees and houses. Fifty-seven people were killed. Within two weeks, ash from the eruption had fallen around the world.

WEST VIRGINIA

NICKNAME:	THE MOUNTAIN STATE
STATEHOOD:	1863
CAPITAL:	CHARLESTON
STATE FLOWER:	BIG RHODODENDRON
STATE BIRD:	CARDINAL

WV

Big rhododendron

Cardinal

If there is a West Virginia, are there also North, South, and East Virginias?

Nope, just a West Virginia. The state was born when Virginia left the Union during the Civil War. The people in the western part of the state wanted to stay with the Union, so West Virginians formed their own state.

How do you build an airport on top of a mountain?

You chop off its top! To build the Charleston airport, workers had to chop the tops off mountains and fill in the surrounding valleys with tons of dirt to make an area flat enough for airplanes.

John Henry vs. a machine. Who won?

West Virginia folktales tell of a railroad worker named John Henry. Henry was a real man, a super-strong African American who pounded spikes into railroad ties faster than anyone alive. Once he tried to pound faster than a mechanical drill—and he succeeded. But he died later that night.

What potential miner disaster is no minor disaster?

Coal mining has been the Mountain State's main industry for more than a hundred years. Being a miner is a dangerous job because mines can collapse and trap workers inside. Miners can also die from black lung disease from breathing in too much coal dust.

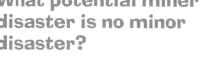

WISCONSIN

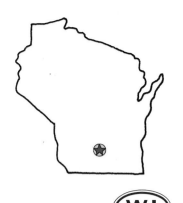

NICKNAME: THE BADGER STATE
STATEHOOD: 1848
CAPITAL: MADISON
STATE FLOWER: WOOD VIOLET
STATE BIRD: ROBIN

WI

Wood violet

What are Holsteins, Jerseys, and Guernseys?

(Here's a hint: When they need to be milked, they mooooooove very slowly.) They're different kinds of cattle. Wisconsin's two million cows make more milk than any other state. The state also produces lots of other dairy products like cheese and butter. No wonder people who live in America's Dairyland are proud to be called Cheese Heads.

Old Wisconsin saying: "The world is your cow, but you'll have to do the milking."

Robin

Test your pioneer skills!

Laura Ingalls Wilder, author of the Little House books, was born in a log cabin near Pepin, Wisconsin, in 1867. She traveled by covered wagon all over the Midwest during her youth, and her books describe pioneer ways on the American frontier. Her first book, *Little House in the Big Woods*, is about growing up in the forest in Wisconsin. Can you match each object below with the item pioneers used to make it?

1. candy
2. doll
3. balloonlike ball

A. corncob
B. pig's bladder
C. snow and molasses

WYOMING

NICKNAME: THE EQUALITY STATE
STATEHOOD: 1890
CAPITAL: CHEYENNE
STATE FLOWER: INDIAN PAINTBRUSH
STATE BIRD: MEADOWLARK

Indian Paintbrush

Meadowlark

Also called the Cowboy State, Wyoming probably has more true working cowboys today than any other state. You might imagine that cowboys live on flat land where nothing changes for miles and miles. But *Wyoming* is a Delaware Indian word that means "alternating valleys and mountains." Wyoming has mountains in the west and plains in the east.

What did Wyoming women get to do before any other American women?

They got to vote, all the way back in 1869! The rest of the country's women didn't get to vote until 1920. Wyoming also had the first woman to serve on a jury, the first female mayor, and the first female governor. No wonder it's called the Equality State.

I *faithfully* shoot ten thousand gallons of hot water more than one hundred feet in the air every eighty minutes, on average. Who am I?

Old Faithful, in Wyoming's Yellowstone National Park, is America's most famous geyser. A geyser is a special kind of hot spring that shoots water into the air. Yellowstone, the world's oldest, largest, and most popular national park, has more than two hundred geysers plus lots of other cool wonders like boiling mud.

Thousands of pioneers traveling west on the Oregon Trail carved their names in a landmark called Independence Rock, near Casper.

WASHINGTON, D.C.
[OR DISTRICT OF COLUMBIA]

NICKNAME: **CAPITAL CITY**
ESTABLISHED: **1800**
FLOWER: **AMERICAN BEAUTY ROSE**
BIRD: **WOOD THRUSH**

DC

Wood thrush

American Beauty rose

Why is Washington, D.C., unlike any other state?

Because it's not a state at all! The District of Columbia (called a district because it's not part of any state, and Columbia for Christopher Columbus) is the capital of the United States. The city is also called Washington, D.C., after President George Washington, who chose the site in 1791 to be the nation's capital.

Who was the only president who didn't live in the White House?

George Washington, who died before it was finished.

Will there ever be a fifty-first state?

There might be, one day. Some people think Washington, D.C., should be the fifty-first state. Others think it should be Puerto Rico, an island territory about nine hundred miles southeast of Florida. We'll just have to wait and see. Who knows? One day the Stars and Stripes may even have fifty-*two* stars on it!

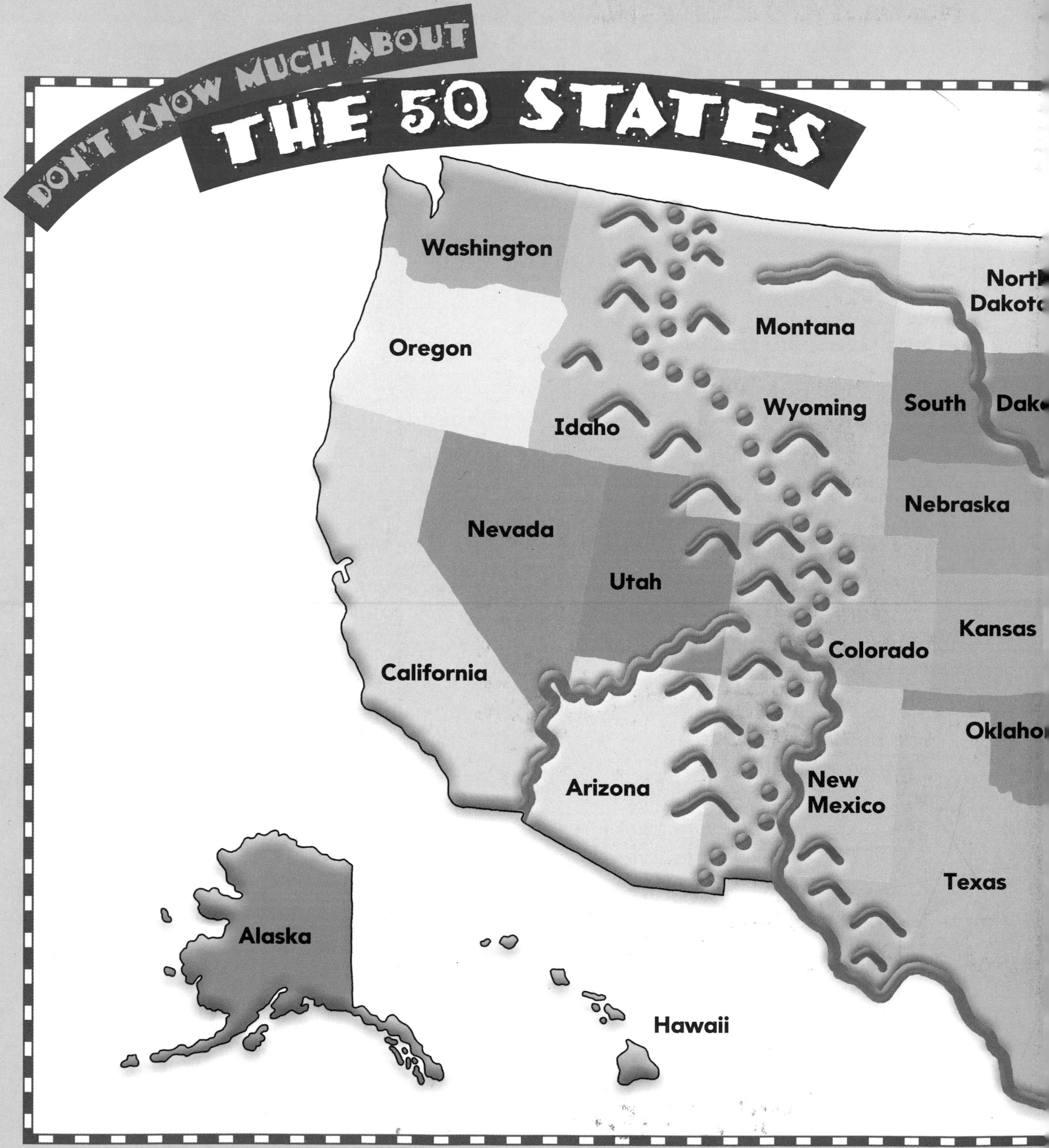

DON'T KNOW MUCH ABOUT
THE 50 STATES
Washington
Oregon
Montana
North Dakota
Idaho
Wyoming
South Dakota
Nebraska
Nevada
Utah
Kansas
Colorado
California
Oklahoma
Arizona
New Mexico
Texas
Alaska
Hawaii

COUNTRY INSIGHTS

JAMAICA

Alison Brownlie

RSVP
RAINTREE
STECK-VAUGHN
PUBLISHERS
The Steck-Vaughn Company

Austin, Texas

COUNTRY INSIGHTS

BRAZIL • CHINA • CUBA • CZECH REPUBLIC • DENMARK • FRANCE
INDIA • JAMAICA • JAPAN • KENYA • MEXICO • PAKISTAN

Title page: Children in front of the statue of Bob Marley, the reggae superstar, in the Park of Fame, Kingston

Contents page: Air Jamaica planes at the airport in Montego Bay, Jamaica

© **Copyright 1998, text, Steck-Vaughn Company**

Published by Raintree Steck-Vaughn Publishers, an imprint of Steck-Vaughn Company

Library of Congress Cataloging-in-Publication Data
Brownlie, Alison.
Jamaica / Alison Brownlie.
    p.   cm.—(Country Insights)
    Includes bibliographical references and index.
    Summary: Introduces the land, climate, history, economy, culture, and people of Jamaica, the third-largest island in the Caribbean Sea.
    ISBN 0-8172-4792-0
    1. Jamaica—Juvenile literature.
    [1. Jamaica.]
    I. Title. II. Series.
F1868.2.B76 1998
972.92—dc21   97-5823

Printed in Italy. Bound in the United States.
1 2 3 4 5 6 7 8 9 0 02 01 00 99 98

Contents

Introducing Jamaica

What picture comes into your mind when you think of Jamaica? Do you imagine white, sandy beaches with palm trees and crystal-clear water? Jamaica does have beautiful beaches, but there are great varieties of other landscapes and people on this small island.

Jamaica is the third largest island in the Caribbean Sea. Its population is made up of people whose ancestors came from all over the world. So the country's food, music, and religions are a mixture of African, Indian, Arab, and European influences.

The first people who lived in Jamaica were the Arawaks. They called the island *Xaymaca*, meaning "land of woods and water," which is how Jamaica got its name. Christopher Columbus and the Spanish arrived in 1494, looking for gold and a route to India. Columbus thought he had reached India, which is why the Caribbean is also known as the West Indies. The Spanish forced the Arawaks to work very hard, and brought new diseases to the island, to which the Arawak had no resistance. As a result they died out quickly.

Beautiful beaches and calm turquoise seas attract many tourists to Jamaica.

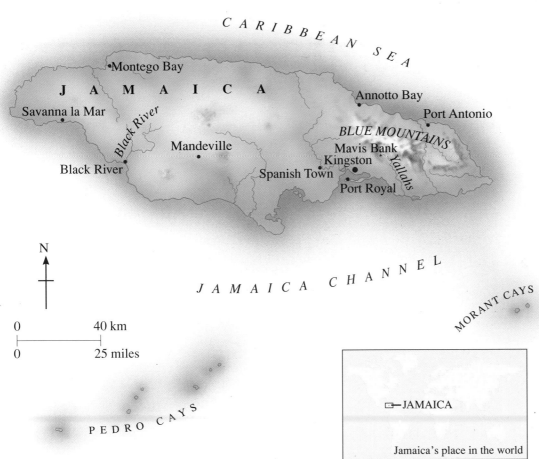

CARIBBEAN SEA

•Montego Bay

JAMAICA

Savanna la Mar

Black River

Annotto Bay

Port Antonio

BLUE MOUNTAINS

Mandeville

Mavis Bank

Kingston

Yallahs

Black River

Spanish Town

Port Royal

N

0   40 km

0   25 miles

JAMAICA CHANNEL

MORANT CAYS

PEDRO CAYS

▭—JAMAICA

Jamaica's place in the world

This book will take you to the city of Kingston and the village of Mavis Bank, as well as to the rest of Jamaica. You can find these places on the map.

▼ Young people make up a high percentage of Jamaica's population.

In 1655 the British (who were interested in growing sugar on the island) took over Jamaica. At first, there were not enough people to work on the land, so the British brought people from Africa to work as slaves. Slavery was abolished in Jamaica in 1807, and Jamaica finally became independent in 1962. Jamaicans are proud of the way in which their ancestors fought against slavery.

JAMAICA FACTS

Population:	2.5 million
Area:	4,244 sq. mi.
Highest mountain:	Blue Mountain Peak (7,402 ft.)
Life expectancy:	74 years
Motto:	"Out of many, one people."

KINGSTON: A MODERN CITY

Kingston is the capital of Jamaica and is a city that teems with life. The pavements are full of street traders selling mangoes, peaches, and sky juice, a sweet fruit liqueur. All kinds of music can be heard on the street corners.

Kingston spreads out across the coastal plain. In the distance you can see the tall buildings of the city's business district.

Like all large cities, Kingston has office buildings, hospitals, banks, and schools. Shops and department stores sell a wide range of goods both made in Jamaica and imported from other countries. Cafés and restaurants sell specialties such as Jamaican patties, alongside Western-style fast food. Kingston also has its fair share of traffic and the traffic jams and pollution that come with it.

Not far from the city center are neighborhoods that have become rundown over the last few years. These areas, such as Trench Town and Jones Town, are dominated by street gangs and have a lot of crime. Lately, however, the government and the people who live there have done much to improve these areas.

PORT ROYAL

The original capital of Jamaica was Port Royal. It was a very popular place with pirates and was known as "the wickedest place in Christendom." In 1693, many people drowned when Port Royal was swamped by a tidal wave following an earthquake.

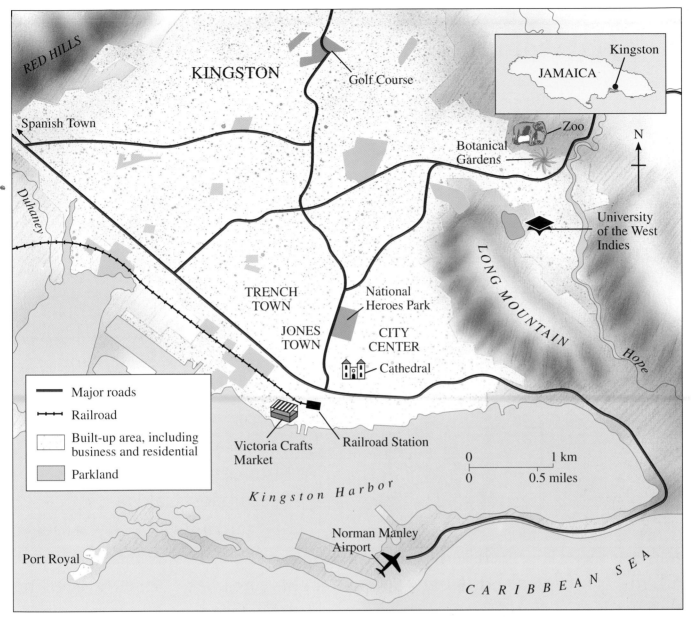

KINGSTON

RED HILLS

Spanish Town

Golf Course

Kingston

JAMAICA

Zoo

Botanical
Gardens

N

Duhaney

University
of the West
Indies

LONG MOUNTAIN

Hope

TRENCH
TOWN

National
Heroes Park

JONES
TOWN

CITY
CENTER

Cathedral

Major roads

Railroad

Built-up area, including
business and residential

Parkland

Victoria Crafts
Market

Railroad Station

0   1 km

0   0.5 miles

Kingston Harbor

Port Royal

Norman Manley
Airport

CARIBBEAN SEA

Kingston has grown very quickly over the last fifty years as Jamaica's population has increased, and many people have moved there looking for work. This has led to the development of factories, which provide jobs and the goods needed in a large city like Kingston.

You can see glimpses of the Blue Mountains from all over the city of Kingston.

THE VILLAGE OF MAVIS BANK

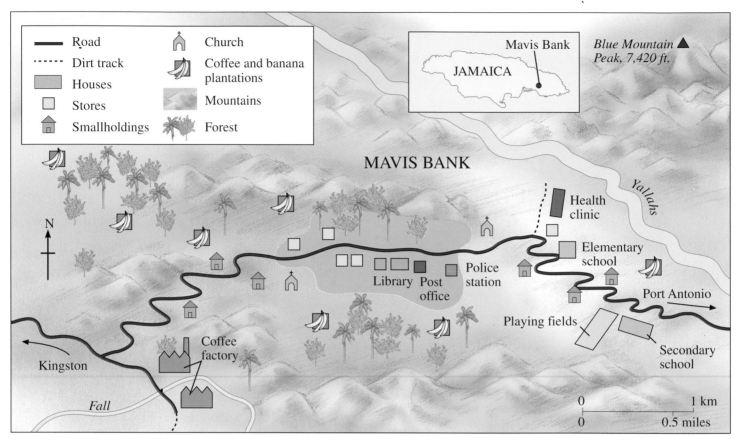

Road
Dirt track
Houses
Stores
Smallholdings
Church
Coffee and banana plantations
Mountains
Forest

JAMAICA
Mavis Bank

Blue Mountain Peak, 7,420 ft.

MAVIS BANK

N

Health clinic
Yallahs
Elementary school
Port Antonio
Police station
Post office
Library
Secondary school
Playing fields

Kingston

Coffee factory

Fall

0   1 km
0   0.5 miles

Mavis Bank is a typical Jamaican village in the parish of St. Andrew's, in the Blue Mountains, just north of Kingston. It hugs the side of the hills, 2,625 ft. above sea level. About 500 people live in Mavis Bank, but the population is spread out. Some villagers live a long way from their nearest neighbors, but most people get around the village by walking.

There is not much traffic on the one road that runs through Mavis Bank.

The village has four churches, three schools, a one-person police station, a post office, and a small library. There are six stores, which sell a few basic products, but they are little more than huts. A nurse runs a small clinic and the doctor visits once a week on Thursday. She travels from Gordon Town, which is about 10 miles away. If someone is ill on any day other than a Thursday, he or she has to travel to Kingston to see a doctor. Medical bills can be very expensive.

The road that runs through Mavis Bank is very steep, winding, and full of pot-holes. Sometimes cars go over the edge of the hairpin bends. Drivers are meant to blow their horns as they go around corners to warn people. The roads are made even more dangerous by streams that run off the mountains and gush across the road. Sometimes parts of the road are washed down the hillside.

Lennox Willis Junior (below left) and his friend at the entrance to Mavis Bank

WELCOME TO THE COMMUNITY OF MAVIS BANK

PROTECT by MBUY

"I was born in Mavis Bank and I really like it here. I'll probably have to go to Kingston though when I am older. There's not much work here."— Lennox Willis Junior 10 years old (left)

9

Land and Climate

Two-thirds of Jamaica is made up of hills and mountains, which are surrounded by flatter, coastal lowlands. The Blue Mountains form the eastern end of a mountain ridge that runs down the middle of the country. Rivers and streams tumble off the hills, often forming waterfalls.

Jamaica's climate is good for farming as well as for attracting tourists. Most of the country is hot all year round, but the Blue Mountains are much cooler. December, January, and February are the coolest months of the year.

The main winds come from the northeast, bringing rain. The north of the island is therefore wetter, greener, and more lush than the south. In some areas of the south, cacti grow. The wettest months are usually from May to October, when tropical downpours can be expected at any time. Heavy rains are a serious problem in Jamaica. It is thought that over 80 million tons of soil are washed away every year in floods.

If you look closely at this picture, which was taken in the Blue Mountains, you can see hairpin turns on one of the roads.

Jamaican crocodiles live in the Black River, Jamaica's longest river. They lurk in the mangroves growing along the banks.

A HARBOR CITY

Kingston is bordered by the Blue Mountains to the north and the Caribbean Sea to the south. The city is slowly creeping up the foothills of the mountains as new suburbs are built. A long peninsula cradles the sheltered lagoon of Kingston Harbor, where you can see ships from all over the world. Long Mountain lies to the east of the city. This is an area of high land where it is too steep to build.

"I like all the sunshine in Kingston, but it's very humid, which makes it quite uncomfortable."—Thelma Jackson, Canadian tourist

Kingston has one of the largest natural harbors in the world.

It is always hot in Kingston. June to September are the hottest months, but it is only a couple of degrees cooler during the rest of the year. The heat causes clouds to form on the mountains behind the city, making them look blue. That is why they are called the Blue Mountains.

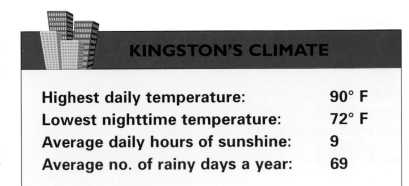

KINGSTON'S CLIMATE

Highest daily temperature:	90° F
Lowest nighttime temperature:	72° F
Average daily hours of sunshine:	9
Average no. of rainy days a year:	69

Most of Kingston's rain falls between the months of May and November. Downpours can be sudden and very heavy. Water runs off the steep slopes of the mountains, and together with heavy rain, turns streets into gushing streams, deep with fast-flowing water. This causes a lot of damage, and there are many potholes and cracks in the roads.

A flooded road just outside Kingston. Flash floods, which turn the roads into rivers of rainwater, make driving difficult at times.

A MOUNTAIN VILLAGE

The steep-sided hills around Mavis Bank are easily eroded by heavy rains.

Mavis Bank lies in the mountains, south of the Blue Mountain Peak. The peak is visible from Mavis Bank, although it is often covered by clouds. Sometimes there is snow on it, but that is very rare.

The Yallahs River starts in the mountains and runs close to the village on its way to the coast. The first people to settle in Mavis Bank chose to live there because the river provided a good source of clean water for drinking and washing. The river has cut a deep gorge into the land, and in places it is difficult to get down to the river. Several small waterfalls have formed where the river flows over rocks. In order to stop the river from eroding the land, walls have been built to hold back the water.

When there is no rain, the river
dries up, leaving a series of
pools where children play.

The soil around Mavis Bank
is fertile, and the climate is ideal
for growing all kinds of crops.
However, the land is very steep, and it is difficult to
find flat ground for farming. Wherever it is possible,
people grow fruit and vegetables. On the rockier,
steeper land they keep goats and chickens.

Mavis Bank is much cooler than Kingston
because it is in the mountains.
The evenings can be chilly,
but people still have no
real need to wear coats.

Inspecting the ▶
ripening coffee
beans on a small
plantation in the
hills above the
village. When the
beans are red, they
are ready to be
picked and sold
to the factory.

Home Life

The family is very important in Jamaica. Children are often raised by a woman on her own, although aunts, grandmothers, and other relations are usually nearby to help. Children have lots of freedom to play, but discipline is strict and children are taught to respect other people. The whole community shares the job of bringing up children, and people help with baby-sitting if the mother is at work. Anyone can scold children if they are misbehaving.

Most people go to church regularly. Even the smallest village has a church, and most have several. In fact, Jamaica has more churches per square mile than any other country in the world. Some Jamaicans follow the Rastafarian religion. Followers of this religion believe that Haile Selassie I from Ethiopia is the Messiah (Jah).

The Anglican church in Black River on a Sunday morning

Nearly everyone speaks English, which is the language children are taught in schools. Many people also speak patois, especially in the hills and country areas. Patois is a mixture of English, African, and other languages.

Jamaican food, like patois, has many influences. It is often spicy, making use of the wide range of peppers that grow on the island. Vegetables such as plantains and breadfruit and fruits such as mangoes and pineapples grow abundantly. In the countryside you can help yourself from the trees.

▼ *A plate of ackee and salt fish, Jamaica's national dish, being served for breakfast.*

TYPICAL JAMAICAN DISHES

Jerk chicken:	**Grilled chicken, prepared with a mixture of peppers, pimiento, nutmeg, and cinnamon**
Festival:	**Deep-fried, sweet corn bread**
Rundown fish:	**Fish cooked with coconut milk and spices**

▲ *Church services are followed by Sunday school for children.*

17

HOME LIFE IN KINGSTON

Kingston is made up of many different neighborhoods. In the suburbs there are leafy avenues of bungalows, surrounded by gardens of tropical plants, and several homes have swimming pools. Often, there are large satellite dishes on the roofs or in the driveways. These are the areas where the wealthier Jamaicans live. Poorer people live in either the shantytowns on the outskirts of the city or in older areas in the city center.

The Smiths live in Red Hills, a suburb to the north of Kingston. Their home is large and has a balcony and a big garden where the children can play basketball.

Mrs. Smith and her three children, from left to right: Kellie-Ann (15), Tariq (11), and Anika (13).

The Smiths have a maid who lives just a short distance away in a small house made of weatherboard with a corrugated-iron roof.

Mrs. Smith shops at the large shopping mall, but many people in Kingston buy their food from the fruit and vegetable stalls in the street markets.

Nearly all the houses in Kingston have electricity and running water, but life is very different in the shantytowns, where the Stephenson family live. The Stephensons live in a house they built themselves, using scrap wood and plastic, and they have no electricity. Their home is built on "captured land," meaning land that does not belong to anyone.

The Smiths' house has a yard where ▶ *the children can play basketball.*

▲ *Even in the wealthy suburbs poor housing exists. The Stephenson family lives in an area like the one in this picture.*

HOME LIFE IN MAVIS BANK

The Willises outside their home in the center of Mavis Bank.

Most of the houses in Mavis Bank are made of concrete and have corrugated-iron roofs. The roofs make a lot of noise when heavy rain falls. All the houses have electricity, and nearly everyone has a television. Only one home in Mavis Bank has a satellite dish.

The Willises and their three children live in a small apartment below the bank. The building is on a small track off the main road and is built into the side of the hill—a common practice in Mavis Bank.

"What I like about Mavis Bank is that everyone knows each other and helps each other out."
—Marion Ferris, schoolteacher

The family has a television, a radio, and a telephone. It is quite dark inside the Willises' living room. The shelves are packed with ornaments, toys, and books. Like the other houses in the village, their home has running water, but if they want hot water they must boil it on the stove.

The stores in Mavis Bank sell items that people need on a day-to-day basis. There are butter, cheese, crackers, canned products, and meats such as pork, chicken, and beef. One store sells farming equipment, including machetes, spades, and fertilizers. If people want to buy clothes or furniture, they must travel to Kingston. The post office at Mavis Bank sorts out the mail, but there are no deliveries. People have to go to the post office to collect their letters.

Jamaica at Work

Jamaica is rich in natural resources. It has fertile land, mineral deposits, and a warm climate. These resources provide many jobs in farming, the mining industry, and tourism.

A large number of Jamaicans work on the land, producing sugar, bananas, and coffee. These crops are sold all over the world. Families also grow many different fruits and vegetables to feed themselves and to sell in local markets.

Edna Brown is a dump truck driver. She is employed by a bauxite mining company and has had this job for nine years.

TYPES OF WORK IN JAMAICA	
	Percentage of working population
Agriculture	25%
Industry	10%
Services	65%

Some Jamaicans work in the bauxite mining industry, extracting bauxite from the ground, using mechanical diggers. Bauxite is a very valuable mineral, known as red gold. It is extracted from the ground as red soil and is then processed with iron to make aluminum. Aluminum is used to make all sorts of different products, from soft drink cans to aircraft wings.

Jamaica has many beautiful beaches and lots of sunshine, so it is easy to understand why many people go there on vacation. Over a million tourists visit the island each year. Tourism creates a huge number of jobs in hotels and restaurants for waiters, cleaners, security guards, and cooks. Some Jamaicans find work as tourist guides, showing visitors around the island. Other people make souvenirs to sell to the tourists.

Many Jamaicans do not have regular jobs. Instead, they do odd jobs here and there. Many people move to the towns to look for work, and some even go abroad.

▲ *Many people are employed in the construction industry in Jamaica. Althea Gordon (above) is working on a new building on the University of the West Indies campus.*

Moving barrels of coffee in a ▶ *coffee factory. The growing and processing of coffee, bananas, and sugar for sale abroad provides many jobs.*

WORKING IN KINGSTON

"The hotel where I work is always busy with tourists from all over the world. I like meeting so many different people all the time."—Winston Johnson, security guard

Many people in Kingston, and from the surrounding region, travel to the city center each day to work in the banks, insurance companies, offices, stores, and factories. They work as managers, secretaries, and computer operators. In factories, people operate machinery producing goods to be sold in Jamaica and abroad.

People travel to work on hot, crowded buses and in private cars, creating traffic jams on the main roads during the rush hour.

The Smiths both have jobs and are well off. Mr. Smith runs his own construction company, building houses, and Mrs. Smith is a real estate agent. They both drive into the center of Kingston every day from their home in the suburbs.

Winston Johnson is a security guard at the Sandhurst Hotel in Kingston. He is employed by a private security firm.

24

People who come to Kingston looking for work are often disappointed. Many find it difficult to find regular employment, so they do whatever work they can. Sheldon Brown is 15 years old. He earns money by washing car windshields while the cars stop at traffic lights. Many women, known as higglers, sell souvenirs and goods such as makeup and hair ornaments on the city's streets. Some higglers even travel to the United States to buy the goods they sell.

On the waterfront people make things to sell to the tourists. There visitors can buy brightly painted wood carvings of Jamaican parrots and fish, printed fabrics, and other colorful souvenirs of their stay on the island.

▲ *Dotty Donaldson on her first day at work at Velma's Gift Shop, on Kingston's waterfront.*

▼ *Sheldon Brown, 15 years old, busy at work in the wealthy suburb of New Kingston*

WORKING IN MAVIS BANK

"On Fridays, I take the bus to Kingston with my baskets of mangoes. I sell them on the streets."—Maria Jarrett, farmer

Jobs where people work from nine to five are unusual in Mavis Bank. Some people make furniture, mend cars, or rent out their cars, but most of these are not permanent jobs.

Nearly every household has a small plot of land on which they grow some of the food they need. Between the rows of fruit, cabbages, and lettuces people also grow six or seven coffee bushes. The beans harvested from these bushes and from larger coffee plantations are sold to the Mavis Bank coffee factory. There the coffee beans are sorted, washed, ground, and packed by the villagers, ready to be sold all over the world.

The amount of work at the coffee factory varies according to the season, so jobs may be available for only a short time.

Packing coffee into foil bags inside the Mavis Bank coffee factory. The factory employs from 150 to 250 people from the village, depending on the season.

Blue Mountain coffee is among the best in the world and is sold to Japan, the United States, and Europe. Mavis Bank is lucky to have the coffee factory, but there are still not enough jobs, and some young people hang around playing dice to pass the time.

Most of the villagers keep a few animals, such as goats and chickens. They let the goats wander during the day or tether them by the side of the road on a narrow stretch of grass.

▲ *Coffee beans being washed at the coffee factory. You can see the Blue Mountain Peak in the distance.*

◀ *One of the shopkeepers in the village. Mavis Bank is a small village, so he knows most of his customers by name.*

Going to School

Almost all children up to the age of 11 years old go to school in Jamaica, and nearly every adult can read and write. The Jamaican school system is considered to be very good. Some people, who have moved abroad to live, send their children back to Jamaica to go to school. However, the government now has less money to spend on schools. As a result, teachers' salaries are low and some schools are overcrowded. In these schools, children have to take turns going to school—some go in the morning and others go in the afternoon.

School usually starts at 8:00 A.M. and finishes by 1:30 P.M., because it is too hot to study in the afternoon. All children wear school uniforms, which their parents must buy, and the teachers are very strict. Jamaicans believe in discipline. Strangers will stop children in the street and ask them why they are not at school. Everyone knows that one of the best ways for children to do well and get on in life is to have a good education.

Children sing the Jamaican national anthem every morning before classes begin.

28

Schoolchildren at ▶ the start of their morning break after the first classes of the day

CLASS SIZE

In Jamaican primary schools, there is an average of one teacher for every 37 pupils.

Places in secondary schools (from 12 years old) are limited, and children have to pass an exam to be accepted. Some poorer children cannot go even if they pass the exam, because they have to help their families by working instead.

Most schools are run by the government, but there are a few private ones where parents must pay and some that are run by the churches. Rastafarian schools teach children about Africa and Marcus Garvey, a Jamaican who fought against racism, as well as their usual subjects.

▼ Young children learn to read and write at an early age. Yannique Brown is five years old and is learning how to write her name.

SCHOOL IN KINGSTON

"I'm on my school's swimming team. We have a really big playing field, where many other games are played."
—John Bennett, 11 years old

There is a greater choice of schools in Kingston than in Mavis Bank. For example, parents can choose to send their children to a single-sex school, which they cannot do out in the country.

Most Kingston schools are better equipped than those in the villages, and the school buildings are more modern. Nearly all of them have computers. A typical high school has about 1,500 pupils. There are usually between 36 and 45 pupils in each class. In more crowded schools, one class may sit facing one way, while a different class faces the other way. In poorer areas, special schools have been set up for younger children, to help them get a better start.

Children share a joke on their way to school in Kingston.

Schools award certificates to pupils for sports achievement, for doing well in school subjects, and also for good citizenship. An example of this is helping people who are less well off than they are.

Students at the University of the West Indies enjoy a quiet moment of study.

Mrs. Smith takes her children to school by car in the morning. The journey takes about half an hour. Many children in Kingston go to school by car, but others walk or take the bus. After school, the Smith children go to a friend's house while their mother is still working. They usually have plenty of homework to do. All the Smith children hope to go to the University of the West Indies in Kingston when they finish school. The university is the largest in the Caribbean.

Passing exams is very important, ▶
and pupils are expected to work hard.

SCHOOL IN MAVIS BANK

In Mavis Bank there is a nursery school for children from three to six years, a primary school for six- to twelve-year-olds, and a secondary school for children from twelve to fifteen years old. The three Willis children walk to school every day. They all go to the primary school, although Todea-Kay will go to the secondary school next year.

Their school is a long, single-story building. Instead of glass there are slats in the windows, which keep out the hot rays of the sun while letting in cool breezes. Even in primary school, children are expected to work hard, and they have about two hours of homework every night.

▼ *Children outside the secondary school in Mavis Bank. The school motto, "Forward for the best," is written in the center of the sign.*

Many pupils stay after school to play soccer on the school's athletic field. This is the only flat piece of land in the village.

The secondary school takes pupils from a wide area. Some children arrive by bus, but others, who live far from the bus route or who cannot afford the fare, must walk. They may have to walk several miles, and it can take some children up to two hours each way. It is difficult for these children to continue to go to school when they live so far away, and are also needed to help at home.

▲ A bus carries children from villages nearby to the schools in Mavis Bank.

"I want to be a nurse when I'm older. I'll have to go to Kingston to go to nursing school."
—Jennifer Brown, 10 years old

Jamaica at Play

Leisure time is very important to Jamaicans. Music, sports, and any event where people can get together are all very popular. Having a barbecue of jerk chicken on the beach, going to a party, or just getting together to talk are essential parts of Jamaican daily life.

Reggae music was born on the island of Jamaica. Bob Marley helped to make this style of music popular all over the world, but it is especially loved by Jamaicans. In the summer, a big reggae festival called "Sunsplash" is held in Montego Bay. Fans travel from all over the world to hear their favorite reggae stars perform. Bob Marley died in 1981, and there is now a statue of him in the Park of Fame in Kingston.

Jamaica's main cultural festival takes place during the weeks leading up to Independence Day in August. Plays are performed all over the island, along with music and dance shows. Everyone is expected to join in!

A billboard and a statue of Bob Marley welcome visitors to "Bob Marley's Jamaica."

Jamaicans are extremely proud of their cultural heritage, but many U.S.-style leisure activities are becoming increasingly popular. That is because Jamaicans watch a lot of American programs on satellite television. Some older Jamaicans are not happy about this and refuse to buy satellite dishes. Even so, U.S. sports such as basketball are played more and more, although cricket is still the country's number one game. Athletic activities are also very popular. For such a small country, Jamaica has been very successful in international track and field events. Merlene Ottey, for example, who is one of the world's best sprinters, has taken part in many competitions and has won medals at two Olympic Games.

▲ *Basketball is growing more and more popular in Jamaica.*

◀ *People talking outside church in Black River on a Sunday morning*

PUBLIC HOLIDAYS IN JAMAICA	
New Year's Day:	January 1
Ash Wednesday:	March/April
Easter Day:	March/April
Labor Day:	May 23
Independence Day:	First Monday in August
National Heroes Day:	Third Monday in October
Christmas Day:	December 25
Boxing Day:	December 26

LEISURE TIME IN KINGSTON

For those who can afford it, every kind of leisure activity is available in Kingston. The capital city has sports stadiums, swimming pools, two drive-in movies, and many theaters. In the shopping malls in the suburbs, there are lots of arcades, where young people like playing video games.

"On weekends, we sometimes go to Hellshire beach for a barbecue. Our whole family goes. That's about 15 people."
—Maria da Costa, supermarket manager

On weekends, people like to forget the noise and crowds of the city by going to the beach or hiking in the mountains. Some people drive up to Mavis Bank and start their trek from there. Others travel all the way to Black River to see the crocodiles.

Playing tennis at the Liguanea Club in New Kingston. This is a private sports club.

◀ *Visitors to Kingston's National Art Gallery look at an exhibition about life in a Kingston shantytown.*

▼ *Children on the grounds of the Kingston YMCA. There are lots of activities to choose from all through the summer vacation.*

Comedies and pantomimes are performed in theaters such as the Ward Theater. These shows are often based on the stories of Anancy, a sly, crafty spider who is the hero of Caribbean fables. Kingston also has a national art gallery and a museum of culture where people can enjoy Jamaica's rich heritage. In the cool of the evenings, people often sit out on their porches talking about the events of the day.

In the center of Kingston and in the poorer areas, there are fewer parks and open spaces where children can play. Instead, they play on the streets or on any empty piece of land they can find.

LEISURE TIME IN MAVIS BANK

If you went to Mavis Bank on a Sunday morning, you would see people on their way to church in their best clothes. Church services include loud, lively singing—everyone joins in! After church, some families go down to the river to swim. Deep bathing pools have been made where villagers have dammed the river.

Music and singing form an important part of church services.

Unlike Kingston, Mavis Bank has no movies or public parks. People make their own entertainment, and children are very good at making the best of what they have. They roll up rags and tie them into bundles to make soccer balls and use small coconuts for cricket balls. The Willis children enjoy making their own games. Lennox Junior makes kites out of bamboo and scrap paper, and Todea-Kay and Natoya play in the streams and woods around their home.

"Sunday after church is a good chance to catch up with everyone."—Cherol Green, 18 years old (left)

Adults gather outside the stores to pass the time of day and catch up on the latest news. Sometimes they chew a small piece of sugarcane while they chat. The pace of life is slow and not much happens.

In the evening most people in Mavis Bank watch television or a video. Miss Patterson, the local librarian, is concerned that people, especially the young, don't read as many books as they used to.

TRADITIONAL TALES

Stories about Anancy, the spiderman, were brought from the west coast of Africa by slaves more than 200 years ago. These stories are often told to children at bedtime.

▲ *Lennox Willis Junior and his friend play with a toy they have made from an old wheel.*

◀ *The Jamaican national flag on the wall of the Mavis Bank library*

39

The Future

Although Jamaica is rich in most resources, it has to import energy, including gasoline for cars and oil for industry. This is very expensive for the country. In the future Jamaica may be able to meet some of its energy needs by using solar and wind power. Some houses already have solar panels and wind pumps, and the government wants to expand their use in the future.

With the increasing use of satellite television, it is likely that the United States will have a greater influence on the Jamaican way of life in the future—the food people eat, the clothes they wear, and the music they listen to. Young people are particularly affected. Some Jamaicans are worried about this trend. Mrs. Smith will not buy a satellite dish because she feels her children should learn more about Jamaican than American culture.

A satellite dish that points toward the United States brings American television programs to Jamaica.

Jamaica has a very young population. Large numbers of these young people no longer wish to work in the countryside but find it difficult to get jobs in town. Some go to live in other countries such as Canada and the United States, where they can earn more money. Unfortunately, those who are well educated, such as teachers, nurses, and doctors, leave Jamaica to find a new life abroad. It is important that these people stay in their country in order to help it develop and prosper in the future.

▲ *A sports shop in New Kingston. Jamaica's athletes continue to rank among the best in the world.*

◄ *A tour boat on the Black River. Tourism is vital to Jamaica's future.*

THE FUTURE OF KINGSTON

Kingston has changed a great deal in the last 20 years. It has grown very quickly, with new office buildings, factories, and suburbs spreading out and up into the foothills. Kingston's rapid growth has made some people better off, but it has also created a large number of poor people, and the gap between the two groups is constantly growing.

Pollution is a problem that faces nearly all large modern cities, and Kingston is no exception. Heavy traffic affects the health of Kingstonians and their ability to get around in their city. On most days smog lies over the city. As more people become wealthier and buy cars, this problem will worsen unless special action is taken.

As the city continues to grow, there is always construction going on somewhere in Kingston.

CITY GROWTH

In just a few years, the Hellshire area has grown from an uninhabited headland to an extension of Kingston. Some people are unhappy that buildings are taking over the natural areas.

As more people come to Kingston in search of jobs, new houses must be built for them. Otherwise the city's shantytowns will keep on growing, along with poverty and crime. However, many projects have been started to make life better for people living in the poorer areas of Kingston. Many young

people from the shantytowns and downtown areas are now being trained in the skills necessary to do some of the new jobs in the city. There are courses that develop computer skills and others that teach people how to run their own businesses. These courses are often taken by people who want to improve their lives.

▼ *Buses in Kingston are usually crowded. Instead of running to a timetable, they set off when they are full.*

43

THE FUTURE OF MAVIS BANK

Unlike Kingston, Mavis Bank has not changed a great deal in the last few years, and some people think it won't change very much in the future. It faces the challenge that all small villages in Jamaica must face—a decreasing population as many young people leave villages to find work in towns and cities. There are a few jobs for young people in the coffee factory, but not enough for everyone. As a result, unemployment is high. Young people are attracted to Kingston not only by the possibility of a job, but also by the "bright lights" and excitement it offers. By comparison, Mavis Bank seems very quiet.

Sorting through coffee beans to make sure only the best are used. The coffee factory will continue to provide much needed work for people in Mavis Bank.

Mavis Bank is not far from Kingston, but the road between the two is in bad condition and the trip can take up to two hours. If the road was improved, more people would be encouraged to live in Mavis Bank because they would be able to travel to Kingston for work.

Some new houses are being built in the village—a sign that people want to live in Mavis Bank—and although many people complain about the cost of living, most are generally better off than they used to be. Nearly every family has a television set, and it is likely that more will get satellite dishes soon.

▲ *Four-wheel-drive vehicles are the best type of transportation on the road between Mavis Bank and Kingston until the potholes and cracks are mended.*

◀ *Lennox Willis Junior and his two friends will probably move to Kingston when they are older, to look for work and excitement.*

45

Glossary

Ancestors The people we are related to who have lived before us, including our grandparents, great-grandparents, and any relatives before them.

Community spirit The way people who live in the same place help one another and work together.

Fertile Fertile land is rich in the nutrients plants need to grow well.

Jerk chicken A traditional Jamaican chicken dish, cooked with lots of spices.

Lagoon An area of water separated from the sea by a sandbank or a piece of land.

Machetes Small axes used to chop wood.

Mangroves Trees and shrubs that grow in mud on riverbanks and on the sea-shore in the tropics. They have long roots that grow above the ground.

Minerals Substances such as gold, coal, and bauxite that occur naturally in the ground and can be obtained by mining.

Pantomime A comic performance or play, usually based on a fairy tale.

Peninsula A piece of land surrounded on three sides by water.

Plantain A fruit that is similar to the banana but tastes less sweet.

Plantation An area of land that is planted with a single crop or type of tree.

Pollution Damage caused to the environment by substances such as poisonous chemicals or toxins from traffic and factories.

Potholes Deep holes in road surfaces.

Racism The belief that one race of people is better than another, and the treatment of others influenced by this belief.

Reggae music Popular West Indian music with the accent on the offbeat.

Resources The things a country possesses that are useful to it. Sunshine, mineral deposits, and people are some of Jamaica's resources.

Self-sufficient Able to supply the things that one needs to live, without help from other people.

Shantytowns Poor areas on the outskirts of cities where people have built their own homes from scrap materials.

Slavery Forced labor for little or no pay. Jamaican slaves belonged to their owners and could be bought and sold. There are still slaves today in some parts of the world.

Solar power A method of obtaining electricity from the heat and light of the sun. It is very expensive to set up but cheap to run.

Souvenirs Objects bought on vacation to remind you of your visit.

Suburbs Areas on the edges of large towns and cities consisting mainly of houses and stores.

Further Information

Books to Read

Hayes, Barbara. *Folk Tales and Fables of the Americas and Pacific*. Folk Tales and Fables. New York: Chelsea House, 1994.

Lerner Publications, Department of Geography Staff. *Jamaica in Pictures*. Visual Geography. Minneapolis, MN: Lerner Publications, 1993.

Mayer, T. W. *The Caribbean and Its People*. People and Places. New York: Thomson Learning, 1995.

Sandak, Cass R. *North America*. Continents. Austin, TX: Raintree Steck-Vaughn, 1997.

Sheehan, Sean. *Jamaica*. Cultures of the World. Tarrytown, NY: Marshall Cavendish, 1993.

Waterlow, Julia. *Islands*. Habitats. New York: Thomson Learning, 1995.

Useful Addresses

Jamaican Embassy
1520 New Hampshire Avenue
Washington, D.C. 20036
202-452-0660

Jamaican Tourist Board
866 Second Avenue
New York, NY 10017
212-688-7650

Sources

All the statistics for this book were taken from the following sources:
UNESCO Statistical Yearbook, 1993;
UN World Statistics in Brief, 14th edition; World Bank World Tables, 1994;
UNICEF, The State of the World's Children, 1995;
UN Human Development Report, 1994.

Acknowledgments

The author would like to thank Nicky Richardson of the Jamaica Tourist Board and Philip Chavannes for information and guidance.

Picture Acknowledgments

All photographs, except those listed below, are by Howard J. Davies.
Page 28, 33 (bottom): Alison Brownlie;
Pages 29, 31 (bottom): Wayland Picture Library (David Cumming).
All maps are by Hardlines.
Border artwork is by Kate Davenport.

Index

Page numbers in **bold** refer to photographs.